A STUDY IN THE BOOK OF JAMES

THRIVE

Living Faithfully in Difficult Times

JENNIFER COWART

Abingdon Women/Nashville

Thrive

Living Faithfully in Difficult Times

ISBN 978-1-7910-2780-3

(*Copyright page continues on page 205.*)

THRIVE

CONTENTS

ABOUT THE AUTHOR

Jennifer Cowart is the executive and teaching pastor at Harvest Church in Warner Robins, Georgia, which she and her husband, Jim, began in 2001. With degrees in Christian education, counseling, and business, Jen oversees a wide variety of ministries and enjoys doing life and ministry with others. As a gifted Bible teacher, Jen brings biblical truth to life through humor, authenticity, and everyday application. She is the author of three women's Bible studies (*Pursued*, *Fierce*, and *Messy People*) and several small group studies coauthored with her husband, Jim, including *The One*, *Grounded in Prayer* and *Living the Five*. They love doing life with their kids, Alyssa, Josh, Andrew, and Hannah.

Follow Jen:

 jimandjennifercowart

 jimandjennifer.cowart

Website: jennifercowart.org or jimandjennifercowart.org

INTRODUCTION

Hi, friend! Welcome to *Thrive*!

Isn't that a great word? *Thrive* describes something alive, vibrant, and moving in the right direction. The word means to prosper or flourish. When we use *thrive* to describe something such as a baby, marriage, business, or church, we are saying that it is healthy and growing—that strength and vitality are present. Are you thriving right now? I really hope so!

As you begin this study, I hope that you are in a fun and fulfilling season of life, one where you are thriving. But not every season feels that way. Sometimes life is hard and you struggle just to get through each day. In those seasons, instead of thriving you are surviving. And when you're in survival mode, the idea of thriving can seem very far away. We've all been in survival mode before, and it's not a great place to be. The place you want to live is where you can thrive!

Great news: No matter where you are in life right now, this study will help you develop six key habits necessary to thrive despite your circumstances: endurance, wisdom, action, control, humility, and prayer. Together we will dig into the Book of James. This letter written in the first century was an instructional gift to believers about how to endure hardships and move beyond survival to a position where they could grow despite a climate of persecution.

One of the ways I love to teach the Bible is verse by verse, also known as expository teaching. However, because James's practical instructions in this book often jump from one topic to another, making it challenging to move fluidly through the letter, we will do some intentional bobbing and weaving as we focus on selected verses according to six overarching themes.

As we make our thematic journey through this five-chapter book—examining and sometimes reexamining specific verses—we'll see that the words James wrote approximately two thousand years ago have very practical implications for us today. In fact, because it's relatively short and an easy read, you might find it helpful to read through the entire book before you begin this study, giving you an overview of James's message. (Chapter summaries are also available on pages 196-200 of this book.)

This workbook contains six weeks of devotional Bible lessons, with five lessons for each week. I call them devotional Bible lessons because they include both Scripture study as well as reflection and prayer. The idea is to give yourself time to savor God's Word and allow Him to speak to you. You may want to find a quiet place where you can do your lessons each day.

As mentioned, the weeks are organized by six overarching themes or habits drawn from James's instruction. Each day the lesson follows the same format:

Settle: As you begin each lesson, I encourage you to just be still for a few moments and allow your heart and mind to settle. In Psalm 46:10 we are told, "Be still, and know that I am God!" In the fast-paced world in which most of us operate, being still, breathing deeply, and resting in God's presence can be challenging. So, as you begin each day's lesson, I encourage you to give yourself the sweet treasure of settling your heart, mind, and soul into your heavenly Father's presence. This alone can be a life-changer as you go through the study!

Focus: Next, focus your mind on God's Word, reading a passage from James and other supplemental Scriptures. Isaiah 55:10-11 (TLB) has a promise for those who dwell on God's Word:

As the rain and snow come down from heaven and stay upon the ground to water the earth, and cause the grain to grow and to produce seed for the farmer and bread for the hungry, so also is my word. I send it out, and it always produces fruit. It shall accomplish all I want it to and prosper everywhere I send it.

Reflect: Now it's time to dig into the Scripture and think about how it speaks into your life. God's Word is so rich, and the practical instruction James offers has much to teach us. As you consider the wisdom he offered to persecuted believers long ago, invite God to give you fresh insights to enrich your life. Space is provided for recording your responses and completing exercises.

Pray: Finally, be still once again and enter into a time of prayer, asking the Holy Spirit to speak personal messages of peace and wisdom into your life. In addition to written prayer starters, I have sprinkled in a few prayer suggestions each week to help you keep your time with God fresh and interesting.

As you begin and end each day's lesson, I encourage you to be creative in your approach to connecting with God. He is a creative genius; just look at all the colors of the rainbow! Obviously, God likes variety and creativity. So, at times I will encourage you to try some new things in the Settle and Pray segments of the lessons. For instance, if you're musical, you may want to begin by singing or playing an instrument. If you're artistic, you may want to end each day by sketching or painting. Perhaps your gift is the written word; then journal what God is speaking to you. You also may want to incorporate praise and worship music (I have included a few song suggestions, but feel free to choose your own), as well as dance or stretching or other physical activity into your devotional study time. Be creative! Think outside your usual practices and try something new.

Before you get started, gather all the supplies you'll need: your Bible, this workbook, a pen or pencil, and any items you need for creative expression—such as a journal, a sketch pad, an instrument, or a device and playlist. Have your tools easily accessible so that nothing deters you from your time with God. Another trick I've found helpful is to have a notepad handy so that if your thoughts begin to drift to things you need to do later, you can just jot them down so they don't divert your focus.

Friends, I have spent far too many days of my life in survival mode. Those seasons are tough, and it's not a very fun way to live. Instead, I want to thrive—don't you? Let's do it— let's get so close to Jesus that we can face whatever comes our way with the attitude that we are going to thrive!

Let's thrive,

Jen

ENDURANCE

Embracing Obstacles as a Means to Maturity

Memory Verse

Dear brothers and sisters, when troubles of any kind come your way, consider it an opportunity for great joy. For you know that when your faith is tested, your endurance has a chance to grow.

James 1:2-3

DAY 1

SETTLE

Spend a few moments quietly before the Lord. Take a deep breath in and then slowly exhale. As you sit in the silence, ask God to use the time you spend with Him over the next six weeks to help you know Him in new and exciting ways.

FOCUS

This letter is from James, a slave of God and of the Lord Jesus Christ. I am writing to the "twelve tribes"—Jewish believers scattered abroad. Greetings!

(James 1:1)

When Jesus had finished these parables, he moved on from there. Coming to his hometown, he began teaching the people in their synagogue, and they were amazed. "Where did this man get this wisdom and these miraculous powers?" they asked. "Isn't this the carpenter's son? Isn't his mother's name Mary, and aren't his brothers James, Joseph, Simon and Judas? Aren't all his sisters with us? Where then did this man get all these things?" And they took offense at him.

But Jesus said to them, "A prophet is not without honor except in his own town and in his own home."

And he did not do many miracles there because of their lack of faith.

(Matthew 13:53-58 NIV)

"Is not this the carpenter, the son of Mary and brother of James and Joses and Judas and Simon? And are not his sisters here with us?" And they took offense at him.

(Mark 6:3 ESV)

After this, Jesus traveled around Galilee. He wanted to stay out of Judea, where the Jewish leaders were plotting his death. But soon it was time for the Jewish Festival of Shelters, and Jesus' brothers said to him, "Leave here and go to Judea, where your followers can see your miracles! You can't become famous if you hide like this! If you can do such wonderful things, show yourself to the world!" For even his brothers didn't believe in him.

(John 7:1-5)

REFLECT

This week as we begin our thematic journey through the New Testament Book of James, we will be camping out in the first four verses of the letter and considering the habit of endurance. But before we dive into our first theme, let's take a look at the first verse and consider the author.

According to James 1:1 (page 11), who wrote this letter?

The letter tells us that James himself wrote it. But which James? There are three notable men who share this name mentioned in the New Testament. So, let's take a quick look at who they are and identify our writer.

First, we see James the brother of John and son of Zebedee, who was among the first disciples Jesus called to follow him. Also known as the Sons of Thunder, this James and his brother, John, were fishermen and major players in the Gospel stories. Among the disciples, this James was part of the inner circle of those closest to Jesus, which also included his brother, John, and Peter. Another notable fact concerning this disciple James is that he was the first of the apostles martyred for his faith.

Next, we see James the son of Alpheus, also one of the original twelve disciples, who is sometimes referred to as James the Less. Although he was present at the major events of Jesus's ministry— such as the feeding of the five thousand, Jesus walking on the water, many healing miracles, and even the ascension of the Lord—we don't actually see him singled out in any particular situation.

Lastly, there is James the brother of Jesus—or, to be more precise, the half-brother, since they were begotten by different fathers (Holy Spirit for Jesus and Joseph for

James). So, which James wrote this letter that was widely circulated to the first-century church?

Although there is some debate among scholars, traditionally the authorship of this book has been credited to James the half-brother of Jesus. As the second-born son to Mary,[1] James grew up in the same household as Jesus. They would have known each other intimately. Surely as boys Jesus and James played together and did chores alongside each other. They must have shared meals at the same table and likely slept in the same room. They were the two oldest children of the household, so it would have been their responsibility to set the example for their siblings.

James knew Jesus well. They were family. Yet, as we've read today, it is clear that Jesus's brothers did not believe He was the Son of God, at least not at first.

My son Josh had the opportunity to lead a Bible study while in college. He invited a random crowd of peers to his apartment and ended up hosting a group of students who, by and large, had grown up in church. Most of them knew the Bible stories and had been to vacation Bible school, but they did not seem to have a personal relationship with Christ. So, Josh chose to lead them through the Book of James. When I asked him why he chose that book, he said this:

> Well, a couple of reasons. One, it's practical and straightforward. There is a lot of life application in there. But mainly, I figured if James grew up surrounded by Jesus and His teachings and still didn't get it, maybe my formerly churched friends could relate to him. I think most of them grew up hearing about Jesus and His teachings too, but they don't believe He is the Son of God. Maybe they need what James needed—to meet the resurrected Christ. Maybe understanding James will lead to the discussion of the need for a personal relationship with Jesus as Lord.

That conversation was profound to me. I wondered how many people have heard about Jesus, done the church thing, and still have never known Jesus as Savior and Lord of their lives in a personal, life-changing way. Many, I would guess.

How many people have heard about Jesus, done the church thing, and still have never known Jesus as Savior and Lord of their lives in a personal, life-changing way?

When you were growing up, what was your understanding of who Jesus is?

Who introduced you to Jesus for the first time?

Review Matthew 13:53-58; Mark 6:3; and John 7:1-5 (pages 11–12). What do you think it would have been like to be one of Jesus's siblings?

James, the unbelieving brother of Jesus, later became the leader of the first-century church in Jerusalem. What a drastic change! How does that kind of life change happen? It happens when a person meets the resurrected Christ in a personal way. Just knowing about the historical figure of Jesus of Nazareth or learning a Sunday school story or even growing up with him isn't enough. To have real life change like James experienced, you have to come to know Jesus as your personal Savior—God's Son, the One who takes away the sins of the world. Surely this is what must have happened to James.

In the first four books of the New Testament, we read many accounts of the life of Jesus, and there is little mention of his family. But what we do read gives us a clear picture that they did not see him as the Son of God. I often have wondered what they thought of Him.

C. S. Lewis, a great writer and theologian, wrote in his classic book *Mere Christianity*, "A man who was merely a man and said the sort of things Jesus said would not be a great moral teacher. He would either be a lunatic—on the level with the man who says he is a poached egg—or else he would be the Devil of Hell. You must make your choice."[2] Perhaps these were the choices Jesus's siblings considered. By rejecting him as Lord, they might have regarded him as either a lunatic or a liar, as Lewis stated, or as a con artist or someone who had delusional thoughts. But as we journey further into the New Testament, we see in Acts that James has had a radical change of heart. He has gone from skeptic to believer.

Though we don't know if Jesus's other siblings had a change of heart, for James there was a drastic turn of faith. This former doubter and skeptic became a leader in the first-century church—in Jerusalem and beyond. The early community of Christians, known as followers of the Way, looked to him for direction, correction, and encouragement.

Read 1 Corinthians 15:3-7. Note those to whom Paul says the risen Jesus appeared.

What do you think James must have felt upon seeing Jesus post-resurrection?

Read Galatians 2:9. What name does Paul, the writer of Ephesians, give to the big three he lists here?

James overcame his doubts regarding who Jesus was. What doubts have you struggled with in your own faith journey?

As James emerged in leadership, the early church faced very challenging times. Persecution had broken out throughout the Roman Empire. Men, women, and even children were hunted and killed for their faith. It was a scary time to be a follower of Christ. So, as a leader of the early church, James wrote this letter to give them guidance and encouragement that would strengthen their faith.

This is a short letter by biblical standards—only 108 verses in five chapters—but it is rich with practical teaching. Contained within this letter is great wisdom for everyday life. Much of it is simple, but as you will soon see, simple does not always mean easy.

If you have not already read through the entirety of James, I encourage you to do so. It won't take you long, and this will give you an overview for our thematic journey through these Scriptures. As we unpack selected verses together over the next six weeks, I hope you will find the words of James to be life-giving. His instructions are not only wise but also filled with encouragement to help you live well—and more than that, to thrive!

PRAY

As we begin this study together, ask God to give you a fresh desire to know Him. Ask Him to show you new dimensions of who He is and to give you a passion to seek Him as the greatest love of your life as never before.

DAY 2

SETTLE

As you begin your time with the Lord today, put yourself in a different physical position. You may want to kneel, place your hands over your face, lie on the floor, or stand with outstretched arms. Try a new posture before the Lord and ask Him to meet you in a new way during your time together today.

FOCUS

Dear brothers and sisters, when troubles of any kind come your way, consider it an opportunity for great joy. For you know that when your faith is tested, your endurance has a chance to grow.

(James 1:2)

Not only that, but we rejoice in our sufferings, knowing that suffering produces endurance, and endurance produces character, and character produces hope, and hope does not put us to shame, because God's love has been poured into our hearts through the Holy Spirit who has been given to us.

(Romans 5:3-5 ESV)

And we know that for those who love God all things work together for good, for those who are called according to his purpose.

(Romans 8:28 ESV)

REFLECT

It is summer as I'm writing this, and my husband, Jim, and I have planted some tomatoes. In the past we haven't had much luck with vegetables, but Jim loves a ripe tomato sandwich, so we thought we'd give it another try. At the end of the first week, our little plants had doubled in size. Now just two weeks after planting, there are signs of flowering buds where juicy red tomatoes will soon be. Those little plants are thriving!

I love to watch things grow. Whether it's children, plants, friendships, churches, stocks, or something else—growth is exciting. It usually indicates health. It's what I want for my life, and it's what I pray for yours—that you would thrive! But what does that mean? Let's define it.

In the context of this study, thriving is living in the sweet spot of God's will. It is being in a right relationship with God so that, no matter the circumstances, we can grow more and more into the likeness of Christ.

Thriving when things are going well is easily doable. For my tomatoes, there has been a good bit of rain and lots of sun in the first two weeks, and as a result there is a lot of growth.

> **Think back to a time of life when you felt like you were thriving. What were the conditions of your circumstances, and how did they affect you?**

> **What conditions help you thrive spiritually?**

With sun and rain, my tomato plants are thriving, but what will happen to them if conditions aren't so favorable? Will they be able to thrive then? And what about us? How can we thrive when conditions are not favorable—when troubles come?

Our memory verse for this week is James 1:2: "Dear brothers and sisters, when troubles of any kind come your way, consider it an opportunity for great joy."

What? Pure joy? Is that how you feel when troubles come your way? Probably not, because if you're like me, my first reaction to problems could rarely be described as joy—and when I say rarely, I mean almost never. When troubles come my way, I don't like it. Do you? If you do, you're either a little weird or vastly more spiritual than I!

When have you experienced a difficult season of life, and what was your first reaction to it?

Let's circle back to the author of the book we're studying, James. As we learned yesterday, James had a dramatic faith shift after meeting Jesus post-resurrection (1 Corinthians 15:7). James personally saw his resurrected older brother, and the proof was overwhelming. His fears were resolved. James came to know Jesus not only as a sibling but also as Lord, the Son of God, his own personal Savior. Personally, meeting the resurrected Christ has a way of easing doubts and fortifying faith. James became a believer. In fact, as we've seen, he emerged as a leader of this new faith movement known as The Way.

In Acts 1–12 we see that Peter, one the of the three disciples closest to Jesus, took on the initial role of leader in the new and rapidly expanding Christian movement. But after Peter's imprisonment and angelic jailbreak, which we read about in Acts 12, the Roman guard began to search for Peter and couldn't find him. We hear little from Peter from this point on in the book of Acts, though we know he continued to carry on ministry as we read about in the letters 1 and 2 Peter. It was under these conditions that a new leader was needed. James the brother of Jesus emerged as the head of the church in Jerusalem.

It was around this same time that persecution began, with sporadic and locally intense persecution of Christians spreading throughout the Roman Empire. Emperor Nero declared Christianity altogether illegal by AD 64,[3] and most believers lived out their faith quietly. It was a scary time to be a follower of Christ. In Acts 12 we see the first of the original disciples martyred: James the brother of John (not Jesus's brother). When Herod saw how the crowds were pleased at the disciple James's death, he had Peter arrested as well, as we've noted. After that, full-scale persecution followed.

> **Read Acts 12. In this power-packed chapter, a great deal happens that affects the Christian movement. Note the significant events here:**

It was in this environment of persecution that James took time to write this letter in hopes that it would give strength and direction to the followers of Christ. It is a letter that starts and finishes strong. Few words are wasted. James was intent to get right to the heart of the matter.

Let's break down his opening comments. He begins, "Dear brothers and sisters" (James 1:1). In other words, "To those of you who share my love for Christ." He continues, "When troubles of any kind come your way" (James 1:2).

Now, let's stop right there. Wouldn't it be nice if we could replace the word *whenever* with *if*? But James doesn't say, "If troubles come our way." He uses the word *whenever* because it is not a matter of if but when. Every living person experiences difficulties. There is no escaping struggles in the human condition. Instead of hoping that we never experience troubles, we would better spend our time preparing for when they come our way.

Picking up again with verse 2, James writes, "When troubles of any kind come your way, consider it an opportunity for great joy."

It is a mature person who can be in a difficult circumstance and recognize the opportunity it presents for growth. And it's an advanced maneuver of a mature person to actually feel joy while in the struggle, knowing that God will do something amazing despite the pain if you turn to him.

Looking back on some of the more stressful times in my life, I can see in hindsight the work God was doing to stretch and grow me. At the time, however, it was just hard, often painful. At the time there were tears. There was anxiety. But in my pain, God was at work. Although He did not cause the stressful situations I've endured, He has been at work in them; and now I can see that God has used so many of my past struggles to develop my faith and strengthen my character.

Romans 5:3-5 (ESV) tells us that we can "rejoice in our sufferings, knowing that suffering produces endurance, and endurance produces character, and character produces hope, and hope does not put us to shame, because God's love has been poured into our hearts through the Holy Spirit who has been given to us."

James knew this passage to be true. The difficult circumstances for first-century believers presented the opportunity for them to draw close to the Lord, lean on one another, and allow their newfound faith to be strengthened. But they had to permit God to work in them in those moments, and in order to do that, they had to endure the troubles with faith.

We face crises of our own, and as we will see later this week, these moments give us the opportunity to allow our character to be refined. The key is to turn to Jesus in our troubles. Our troubles present a unique circumstance conducive to growth, one in which we can move past our fears and doubts and embrace Him in the pain.

Think again of the difficult time you named earlier. As you look back on it now, what did you learn from it?

Has there been a difficult season when you turned to the Lord for peace and help? If so, how did that time affect your faith?

Back to my tomato plants. Due to the perfect conditions of sun and rain in these first two weeks, our tomatoes have had a good start. But what will be even more impressive is if they endure the times when there isn't enough rain, and the Georgia summer sun is beating down on them. If they can thrive in those conditions, with a little help from us, well, that will be even more exciting. Because thriving in the face of obstacles shows fortitude. And if those tomatoes thrive through a tough summer, they may just taste sweeter when they're ripe.

The same thing can happen for us. As you endure your tough seasons with faith, there is often a deep peace and sweet fruit that will be produced through that perseverance. Press on, friends, so that you can thrive!

PRAY

As you pray, reflect again on Romans 8:28 (ESV):

And we know that for those who love God all things work together for good, for those who are called according to his purpose.

Lord, thank You for being with me in my struggles. Help me to see them as opportunities to lean on You and seek You in new ways. As others watch my life, may I be a light of joy despite whatever circumstances I may be facing. Thank You, Lord, for peace in the storm and Your presence in my pain. Amen.

As you endure your tough seasons with faith, there is often a deep peace and sweet fruit that will be produced through that perseverance.

DAY 3

SETTLE

Listen to a song that brings you peace as you quiet your heart today. It may be a song from childhood or a hymn or worship song that has come to have special meaning to you. Allow the words to wash over you and bring you a sense of calm before the Lord as you seek Him.

FOCUS

Dear brothers and sisters, when troubles of any kind come your way, consider it an opportunity for great joy. For you know that when your faith is tested, your endurance has a chance to grow. So let it grow, for when your endurance is fully developed, you will be perfect and complete, needing nothing.

(James 1:2-3)

Praise be to the God and Father of our Lord Jesus Christ, the Father of compassion and the God of all comfort, who comforts us in all our troubles, so that we can comfort those in any trouble with the comfort we ourselves receive from God. For just as we share abundantly in the sufferings of Christ, so also our comfort abounds through Christ. If we are distressed, it is for your comfort and salvation; if we are comforted, it is for your comfort, which produces in you patient endurance of the same sufferings we suffer. And our hope for you is firm, because we know that just as you share in our sufferings, so also you share in our comfort.

(2 Corinthians 1:3-7 NIV)

Friends, when life gets really difficult, don't jump to the conclusion that God isn't on the job. Instead, be glad that you are in the very thick of what Christ experienced. This is a spiritual refining process, with glory just around the corner.

(1 Peter 4:12-13 MSG)

REFLECT

Life is full of unexpected moments.

In talking with my son's fiancée, Hannah, a few weeks before their wedding, I encouraged her not to be too disappointed when—not if—something went wrong the weekend of the big event. "Something always happens," I told her. "But don't worry. As long as you two are there and you have the pastor [who happened to be my husband!] and the license, all will be fine! So again, not if but when something happens, let's all just smile and make the best of it."

Fast-forward to the weekend of their wedding. It was a beach destination ceremony. We arrived early, and the entire family and bridal party were staying in a house together. Then it happened—the thing none of us expected that threw a wrench into the festivities. And it was me!

After remaining COVID-19 negative for two years throughout the pandemic, I woke up at 4:00 a.m. on the day of the rehearsal dinner with the symptoms. After two years of masking and washing my hands, two years of caring for others but never being sick myself, it was my turn. A quick test confirmed my fear: I was the wrench. It was not what we expected or wanted, and all being in a house together with nowhere to go made being sick and staying isolated challenging. What would we do?

As I lay there at 4:00 a.m. exploring my options, I realized that I was about to miss most, if not all, of my son's special weekend. The sadness came like a wave. The anxiety like a typhoon. Who would handle things? What all would I miss? The questions kept coming.

As I lay there overwhelmed with what this would mean for us, I began to cry out to the Lord. And, friend, I'm going to get honest with you: I was upset. I asked the Lord, "What did I do? Is this a punishment? Do you see me? Are you paying attention? Is this my fault? Please, God, not now!" My emotions were everywhere—and so were my questions.

But then, there was peace.

Now don't misunderstand me, in the peace there were still questions. The night before I realized I was sick, I had been with my parents. Had I infected them? What about the bride and groom? Were they okay? I'd been all over the place the last few days. Who might I have infected? A few hours later when Jim started coughing, I knew I was not the only wrench.

It wasn't what we wanted for our son's special day. But there was nothing I could do to change the circumstances. In those early-morning moments, as I lay there waiting to send a text that would shake my family, God spoke to me. He said, "Look out the window. You have the perfect view of where the ceremony will be. You won't miss much." And then He said, "Jen, you may miss some things this weekend, but they love you. You may miss some of the wedding, but you will be present to watch the marriage, and that's where the real magic happens." Then there was peace in my little storm.

The advice I'd given to sweet Hannah was advice that I now had to embrace. So, despite feeling terrible, I stood on a balcony and waved to my son with a smile plastered on my face. This wasn't what we wanted, but we would get through it.

The entire weekend was bittersweet. I was disappointed, my son was stressed, and my husband was sick; and when my dad began to cough, I was concerned at a new level. But God was present. He kept reminding me, "Life is messy. Don't get bitter. Keep smiling, it's going to be okay." We all recovered, by the way, and the pictures are beautiful.

I intentionally had to remind myself that sometimes life just happens. Even when it's not what we want, God is still on the job. He hasn't abandoned us. In fact, the only place to find peace in those moments is in Him.

When has life not turned out as you dreamed?

When that happened, what was your first response?

What would you like your first response to adversity to be?

As you've faced problems in life, what questions have you had for God?

Yesterday we dug into the first few verses of James. Today we will revisit those verses and add to them these powerful words from the apostle Peter:

Friends, when life gets really difficult, don't jump to the conclusion that God isn't on the job. Instead, be glad that you are in the very thick of what Christ experienced. This is a spiritual refining process, with glory just around the corner.

(1 Peter 4:12-13 MSG)

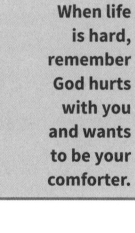

When life is hard, remember God hurts with you and wants to be your comforter.

James does not say that we must rejoice *for* the problems in our lives, but that we can choose to rejoice *in* them. There is a huge difference. Honestly, when I'm talking with someone who is facing a tragedy such as the death of a spouse, a miscarriage, or something horrific like rape, the idea of telling them to rejoice in the opportunity for growth seems completely inappropriate. Finding any joy in moments like that is so very hard to do. However, there is something so precious about leaning heavily into God's presence in our pain and then allowing His comforting peace to flood over us.

Reread 2 Corinthians 1:3-7 (page 23). What does this passage tell us to do in times of trouble?

What are some ways God has comforted you during difficult seasons?

How has that prepared you to comfort others?

Today we have read passages from James, Peter, and Paul, three of the greatest leaders of the early church. A common theme from each of these passages, as well as throughout the New Testament, is that troubles are a part of life. The faith of first-century Christians left them under constant threat of death. James, Peter, and Paul wrote to encourage believers then and now. Their instruction is to take courage during times of suffering and look for God to make Himself known in the pain.

When life is hard, remember God hurts with you and wants to be your comforter. If you will turn to Him in your pain, He can use that hurt to develop your character and produce in you a deeper level of spiritual maturity. Friend, know that God is present and wants to help you thrive, even in the hardest times of life.

I don't know what pain you've been through, but I do know that God loves you, and if you will allow it, He can use those times of pain to strengthen your faith. Know this today: You are loved; the God of the universe smiles upon you and wants the best for your life!

PRAY

Dear God, You know my hurts. You know the pain I continue to carry. Would You heal me and grow me into the person You created me to be? I love You, and I need You! Amen.

DAY 4

SETTLE

Stand up and take a deep breath in. As you exhale, release the troubles you've been carrying. Now, do it again. At least for the duration of this time with the Lord, lay those troubles to the side and give God your full attention. (It may just be that you choose not to pick up those burdens as you close today, too!)

FOCUS

Consider it a sheer gift, friends, when tests and challenges come at you from all sides. You know that under pressure, your faith-life is forced into the open and shows its true colors. So don't try to get out of anything prematurely. Let it do its work so you become mature and well-developed, not deficient in any way.

(James 1:2-4 MSG)

You have tested us, O God;
*   you have purified us like silver.*
*   (Psalm 66:10)*

I have refined you, but not as silver is refined.
*   Rather, I have refined you in the furnace of suffering.*
*   (Isaiah 48:10)*

"It will come about in all the land,"
Declares the Lord,
"That two parts in it will be cut off and perish;
But the third will be left in it.
And I will bring the third part through the fire,
Refine them as silver is refined,
And test them as gold is tested.

They will call on My name,
And I will answer them;
I will say, 'They are My people,'
And they will say, 'The LORD is my God.'"

(Zechariah 13:8-9 NASB)

REFLECT

Early in our marriage, my father-in-law gave my husband, Jim, and me some valuable advice. He said, "You two are going to need to toughen up. You can't bleed every time you get cut in life. You need to develop some spiritual calluses. Every time you get cut, you don't have to bleed out."

We were young and tender. The idea of someone not liking us or talking poorly about us, especially in ministry, left us wounded. It hurt, leaving us disillusioned; and as a result, we would shut down. But shutting down when we faced hard times, or worse, playing victim, didn't do anyone any good. We needed spiritual calluses. We needed maturity. We had to toughen up so that we could face difficult times and endure them with integrity and grace.

So, Jim and I asked God to help us find a spiritual and emotional maturity in how we faced obstacles. And do you know how God accomplished that? It was by putting more obstacles in our path. Ugh! Be careful what you pray for, right?

It was a process that refined us. With each problem, we turned to God, asking Him to stretch us and teach us and not let us miss the opportunity for growth. One of the tragedies of life is wasted opportunities. If we had to endure problems anyway, we wanted God to use them in some way. We didn't want to waste a hurt.

What is something that wounded you in the past?

Read Psalm 34:18. What does this passage tell you about God's attitude toward your wounds?

> **Though God does not cause the fire, God is your refiner when you're in the fire; and He can burn off your impurities so that you can shine in Jesus's likeness.**

The process of refining gold is interesting. Essentially, the gold is melted down so that it separates from everything impure. All the impurities are scraped away so that only what is beautiful and pure remains. In fact, in earlier days, a goldsmith would know the process was complete when he could see his reflection shining in the gold.

This week we've been examining the first few verses of James's letter. The word *test* in verse 3 is the same word used for processing a precious metal. James compares the refining fire for gold to what God wants to achieve in you as you face the problems of life. What great imagery! I like the wording of The Message Bible.

Reread James 1:2-4 from the Message Bible (page 28). What does James say will be the outcome of this test?

Though God does not cause the fire, God is your refiner when you're in the fire; and He can burn off your impurities so that you can shine in Jesus's likeness.

Enduring the refiner's fire—or the test, as James describes it—can leave you stronger, bolder, wiser, and more prepared to be used by God in the future. But when you're in the fire, it's hard! It can be painful and leave you with scars. Yet even your most painful experiences can be used or redeemed by God.

Reflect on your own life. When have you been in the refiner's fire?

What did God produce in your character through that time?

Reread Zechariah 13:8-9 (pages 28–29) and paraphrase it in your own words:

This passage from Zechariah 13, though a tough one, is near and dear to my heart. In those early years of ministry, when life was hard, a man we had never met before walked up to Jim and me and handed us a note that had this passage on it. He said, "I hope you don't think this too odd, but God has not forgotten you. What you're going through has a purpose. Allow it to strengthen you." Well, it was odd, especially because we were attending a conference in another state and did not know a single person in the room!

It was odd, but it also was incredibly precious and timely. We were experiencing a difficult time, and this was a reminder that in our pain, Jesus was there. He knew what we were going through, and He wanted us to allow Him to use it to strengthen us. We have never seen that man again. But that note, the verse, and his message gave meaning to our troubles. We paid attention. We didn't want to waste the hurt. In fact, we doubled down on Zechariah 13. Then we studied others that echoed the same message, such as those we read today from Psalms and Isaiah:

You have tested us, O God; you have purified us like silver.

(Psalm 66:10)

I have refined you, but not as silver is refined. Rather, I have refined you in the furnace of suffering.

(Isaiah 48:10)

These are not easy verses to embrace. Going through the refiner's fire is difficult. Watching our children and loved ones go through the fire is painful. But it's through the fire that imperfections are burned away and something beautiful and clean is created.

When I or my family have faced a challenge, all too often I have just wanted it to end. But as James explains, if troubles end prematurely, we may miss the lesson (1:4). We must allow the fire to do the refining if we want to come out the other side purified, as Psalm 66:10 describes.

Life can be hard. In fact, some seasons can seem absolutely overwhelming. But in those times of suffering, as James reminds us, we have the opportunity to grow.

How might God be inviting you to not waste your hurt?

How might you turn the pain of your past into a ministry to others?

Troubles—or suffering, as the prophet Isaiah describes it (48:10)—are where our character can be developed, where we can be refined by the fire. It's where impurities are exposed, melted down, and if we allow it, scraped away by the Refiner so that we can thrive!

PRAY

Cry out to God in your own words, asking Him to help you recognize the opportunities present in times of trouble. Thank Him in advance for what He will do in your character through your current struggles.

DAY 5

SETTLE

Gratitude is a powerful feeling. In fact, it's hard to be sad when you focus on being grateful. As an act of worship, begin your time with the Lord by writing down ten things for which you are deeply grateful, and then simply reflect on the goodness God has brought into your life.

FOCUS

James, servant of God and of the Lord Jesus Christ, sends greetings to the twelve dispersed tribes. When all kinds of trials and temptations crowd into your lives my brothers, don't resent them as intruders, but welcome them as friends! Realise that they come to test your faith and to produce in you the quality of endurance. But let the process go on until that endurance is fully developed, and you will find you have become men of mature character with the right sort of independence.

(James 1:1-4 Phillips)

We are pressed on every side by troubles, but not crushed and broken. We are perplexed because we don't know why things happen as they do, but we don't give up and quit. We are hunted down, but God never abandons us. We get knocked down, but we get up again and keep going. These bodies of ours are constantly facing death just as Jesus did; so it is clear to all that it is only the living Christ within who keeps us safe.

Yes, we live under constant danger to our lives because we serve the Lord, but this gives us constant opportunities to show forth the power of Jesus Christ within our dying bodies. Because of our preaching we face death, but it has resulted in eternal life for you.

We boldly say what we believe, trusting God to care for us, just as the psalm writer did when he said, "I believe and therefore I speak." We know that the same

God who brought the Lord Jesus back from death will also bring us back to life again with Jesus and present us to him along with you. These sufferings of ours are for your benefit. And the more of you who are won to Christ, the more there are to thank him for his great kindness, and the more the Lord is glorified.

That is why we never give up. Though our bodies are dying, our inner strength in the Lord is growing every day. These troubles and sufferings of ours are, after all, quite small and won't last very long. Yet this short time of distress will result in God's richest blessing upon us forever and ever! So we do not look at what we can see right now, the troubles all around us, but we look forward to the joys in heaven which we have not yet seen. The troubles will soon be over, but the joys to come will last forever.

(2 Corinthians 4:8-18 TLB)

REFLECT

We've seen this week that James, who based his ministry in Jerusalem, begins his letter by greeting the twelve tribes of Israel scattered among the nations. The persecution of believers, particularly in Jerusalem, escalated the dispersion of believers. Many lost their homes and were afraid for their lives because of the threats they faced as followers of Christ. So, they scattered throughout Israel to protect their families. As we have considered, life as a believer was scary for the audience who first received this letter.

The passage you read today from Paul's second letter to the Corinthians lets us know that the environment in Corinth was very much like that in Jerusalem. Troubles, real life-threatening struggles, were a part of daily life for the early believers. Neither James nor Paul could alter that fact, but they did want to give guidance on the attitudes believers should have as they faced their struggles.

Troubles, real life-threatening struggles, were a part of daily life for the early believers.

> **Reread today's passages (pages 34–35) and record below the attitudes and actions a believer is encouraged to have during times of struggle:**

Have you ever had a friend who always seemed to be dealing with a crisis? I'm not talking about a hypochondriac or a drama queen. I mean someone who really has had more than their fair share of problems. I have a few of those people in my life. They have had more hard knocks than most other people. So, when I read 2 Corinthians 4:17, I think of them: "Our light and momentary troubles are achieving for us an eternal glory that far outweighs them all" (NIV).

This passage is hard to take when you're in the thick of hard times. It's written with an eternal perspective. And in our earthly pain, eternal perspectives can feel elusive. When you are in pain, you rarely think of it as a light and momentary situation.

Personally, I've been through several tough events, but it's the tough seasons that really get me. When it's a death or health crisis, I handle it pretty well; but when tough events become cumulative, that's when it can be overwhelming.

Years ago, I went through one of those long, tough seasons. Everything, I repeat *everything*, seemed hard, and God seemed distant. Joy was elusive. We had moved to a new area to start a church, and the ministry was going really well. People were accepting Christ. My husband was thriving in his new role as a church planter. But I was not.

I worked long hours at his side and focused full-time on both ministry and raising our two little ones. We were doing good work. But I was lonely and felt guilty for not having the joy Jim seemed to have in response to all that was exploding around us. We were healthy, the kids were doing well, the church was growing—what did I have to be sad about? What was wrong with me? Why didn't I feel the joy?

In a time when most people probably thought I was thriving, I was miserable. There was always too much to do, and for some reason I thought I had to be on top of everything. Can you relate?

During this time, I did a few things right:

1. I vowed to make my husband and our children, Alyssa and Joshua, a priority—a decision I have never regretted.

2. I committed my son's nap time hour to the Lord. Every day I would go onto our deck and read Scripture as he slept.

In truth, I couldn't even pray during that time. So, I would just read the Bible. I have no idea what I read, but I would not give up. In a semi-numb state, I would let the words of God wash over me. Every day, as an act of obedience, I would read. But to me it felt like a futile attempt to seek God.

Eventually, life got easier. I gave myself permission to relax a little, and the work became more manageable. Joy began to return. As I look back on that tough season, the surprise is that most of the Scripture I have memorized to this day came from that deck time. God was with me. Although I was oblivious to it at the time, God was using that time to produce something in me that had been very hard in the past—His word was resonating deep within me.

Looking back, I realize it really was a very hard season. Small children, new believers, systems that needed to be developed, so many meetings in our home, and a rotating door of people in crisis kept us far too busy. If I could go back and give my younger self some advice, it would be to relax and be patient with others and myself. I'd say, "Jen, you simply don't have to do everything all at once. Take a breath, go play with the kids, and enjoy this journey."

If you could go back and give your younger self some advice regarding difficult times, what would you tell her?

There are times in life that are just hard. We may think in those moments that God has abandoned us, but friend, that will never happen. When life is hard, remember these three things:

1. Troubles are part of life.

   Read and paraphrase 1 Peter 4:12-13.

2. God is always for you!

   Read and paraphrase Psalm 9:9-10.

3. God wins, so choose joy!

   Read and paraphrase Revelation 21:4.

This week we have focused on how to deal with the inevitable problems of life through endurance. We all have problems. Sometimes they are hard emotionally—such as rejection, depression, and exhaustion. Sometimes they are serious—such as disease, persecution, and abandonment. Sometimes life is just hard. Whatever our circumstances, these opening remarks in the Book of James remind us that we get to choose our attitude. We get to decide whether the problems of life will leave us broken and bitter, or better and beautiful.

Every struggle in life is an opportunity. Don't waste your opportunities, especially the painful ones. Invite God into the midst of each situation and allow Him to produce in you a work that develops your character—and even gives you the courage to use your pain to help someone else in the future. Let's not waste those hurts; let's use them to share Christ and, in doing that, to really see what it means to thrive in tough times.

PRAY

God, forgive me for the opportunities I've wasted in the past, and help me to recognize and seize the ones I face moving forward. Please give me strength and faith to endure difficult times. Lord, grow me. Shape me. Make me into the person You want me to be, because I want to reflect Jesus. I want to thrive! Amen.

Endurance

Embracing Obstacles as a Means to Maturity

Dear brothers and sisters, when troubles of any kind come your way, consider it an opportunity for great joy. For you know that when your faith is tested, your endurance has a chance to grow.

(James 1:2-3)

To _____ means we are _____ or _____.

James writes to _____ believers, to give them encouragement and guidance about how to face the challenges ahead.

It's not _____ trouble comes, it's _____.

2

WISDOM

Having Heavenly Perspective on Earthly Issues

Memory Verse

If any of you lacks wisdom, you should ask God, who gives generously to all without finding fault, and it will be given to you.

(James 1:5 NIV)

DAY 1

SETTLE

Take a few minutes to express your love for God through a creative outlet. Sing, play an instrument, draw, write a poem, or whatever you enjoy. As you create, allow God's presence to fill you with joy. (Even just a few minutes of creativity can infuse us with joy!)

FOCUS

If any of you lacks wisdom, you should ask God, who gives generously to all without finding fault, and it will be given to you.

(James 1:5 NIV)

The teachings of the LORD are perfect;
*   they give new strength.*
The rules of the LORD can be trusted;
*   they make plain people wise.*
*   (Psalm 19:7 NCV)*

Getting wisdom is the wisest thing you can do!
*   (Proverbs 4:7)*

"For my thoughts are not your thoughts,
*   neither are your ways my ways,"*
*   declares the LORD.*
"As the heavens are higher than the earth,
*   so are my ways higher than your ways*
*   and my thoughts than your thoughts."*
*   (Isaiah 55:8-9 NIV)*

Do not deceive yourselves. If any of you think you are wise by the standards of this age, you should become "fools" so that you may become wise. For the wisdom of this world is foolishness in God's sight. As it is written: "He catches the wise in their craftiness."

(1 Corinthians 3:18-19 NIV)

REFLECT

One of the smartest people I've ever known was my high school Sunday school teacher. At first I didn't realize just how brilliant she was. She was just the woman who taught our class. But it didn't take long to realize that this lady was not your average Sunday school teacher! She was one of the superintendents of our school system and was a pretty big deal in town. She held multiple degrees and knew more about the Bible than a bunch of rowdy teenagers could possibly comprehend.

As we got to know her, she earned our love and respect. I don't remember any particular lesson she ever gave us. But I do remember her saying something along these lines: "The more I have learned in my life, the more I realize how little I really know. And what I have learned in books still does not produce wisdom; that comes from God alone."

That was imprinted on my young mind. This brilliant, highly educated woman was telling us that in the big scheme of things, she really didn't know that much. And even with all she knew, that didn't make her wise. All I could think was, Well, then, what hope is there for the rest of us?

That day began my quest to figure out what wisdom was all about.

> **Read the following proverbs and note what you learn about wisdom from each.**
>
> **Proverbs 4:7**
>
>
>
> **Proverbs 8:11**
>
>
>
> **Proverbs 24:5**

How might seeking wisdom impact your life?

The Book of James in the New Testament has amazing similarities to the Old Testament Book of Proverbs. Both are practical and full of instructions on how to live. Both also carry a theme of seeking wisdom.

As Proverbs 4:7 says, "Getting wisdom is the wisest thing you can do!" Now, that's a big statement. More than wealth, success, relationships, or anything else, the Bible says wisdom is the thing you should seek. So, this week, through a focus on verses in the first and third chapters of James, we will explore what wisdom is and how it can impact your life.

A definition of wisdom that I like is seeing the world from God's perspective.

Reread Isaiah 55:8-9 (page 43). According to the prophet Isaiah, how does God's perspective differ from ours?

How would you paraphrase these verses?

People are looking for sources of truth today. Horoscopes, fortune cookies, psychics, and self-help books are all tools people resort to in hopes of finding direction for their lives. But we who know God know that the only true source of hope comes from God and His Word. Psalm 19:7 (NCV) says,

"The teachings of the Lord are perfect; they give new strength. The rules of the Lord can be trusted; they make plain people wise."

I love the last phrase of that scripture: God's wisdom will "make plain people wise." You don't have to be a superstar or have a seminary degree to obtain wisdom. It is available to everyone.

Reread James 1:5 (page 43). According to James, how do we obtain wisdom?

As James says, we need only ask and God is ready to shower wisdom upon those who follow Him. God not only gives us wisdom, He gives it generously.

Who do you consider wise? What sets them apart from others?

How do wisdom and intellect differ? What practical differences are there between one who is smart, knowing a lot of facts, and one who is wise, knowing how to live in a way that pleases God?

With wisdom, plain people become wise. What a wonderful promise from God's word. I have so often watched highly educated people make poor decisions. While their degrees hang on the wall, they make choices that lead to failed marriages, spoiled children, debilitating addictions, and struggling businesses. How does that happen?

It happens when people rely on their own desires and intellect instead of turning to God for wisdom and discernment.

Reread 1 Corinthians 3:18-19 (page 43). How is the wisdom of this world "foolishness" in God's sight?

The wisdom of this world is foolishness in God's sight.

These are verses worth memorizing! The wisdom of this world is foolishness in God's sight. James urges the believers of the first century to pray and ask God for wisdom to know how to live in difficult times. That advice holds true today. God is ready to pour out His wisdom and discernment upon those who love Him. He wants us to live above the fray. God wants us to save ourselves from unnecessary stress and consequences by choosing to live according to His word and in fellowship with Him on a daily basis.

Since my high school Sunday school class, I've gone on to earn several degrees and I have attended many seminars. Education is great, but it does not produce wisdom. That comes from the Lord alone. As my high school Sunday school teacher taught us, no matter how much you may learn, wisdom comes from the Lord. So as Proverbs instructs, get wisdom! It is the most important thing you can do.

PRAY

Ask God for His wisdom and perspective today. Humble yourself before the Lord and allow Him to bless you with His spirit and understanding as you seek Him with your whole heart.

DAY 2

SETTLE

What brings you joy? Singing, drawing, exercising, laughing, gardening—whatever it is, take a few minutes to do that before your time with the Lord, and do it as an offering to the Lord.

FOCUS

If you need wisdom, ask our generous God, and he will give it to you. He will not rebuke you for asking. But when you ask him, be sure that your faith is in God alone. Do not waver, for a person with divided loyalty is as unsettled as a wave of the sea that is blown and tossed by the wind. Such people should not expect to receive anything from the Lord.

(James 1:5-7)

Solomon showed his love for the Lord by walking according to the instructions given him by his father David, except that he offered sacrifices and burned incense on the high places.

(1 Kings 3:3 NIV)

At Gibeon the Lord appeared to Solomon during the night in a dream, and God said, "Ask for whatever you want me to give you."

Solomon answered…

I am only a little child and do not know how to carry out my duties. Your servant is here among the people you have chosen, a great people, too numerous to count or number. So give your servant a discerning heart to govern your people and to distinguish between right and wrong. For who is able to govern this great people of yours?

The Lord was pleased that Solomon had asked for this. So God said to him, "Since you have asked for this and not for long life or wealth for yourself, nor have asked for the death of your enemies but for discernment in administering justice, I will do what you have asked. I will give you a wise and discerning heart, so that there will never have been anyone like you, nor will there ever be.

(1 Kings 3:5-12 NIV)

God gave Solomon wisdom and very great insight, and a breadth of understanding as measureless as the sand on the seashore.... From all nations people came to listen to Solomon's wisdom, sent by all the kings of the world, who had heard of his wisdom.

(1 Kings 4:29, 34 NIV)

*As Solomon grew old, his wives turned his heart after other gods, and his heart was not fully devoted to the L*ord *his God, as the heart of David his father had been.*

(1 Kings 11:4 NIV)

How much better to get wisdom than gold,
and good judgment than silver!
(Proverbs 16:16)

REFLECT

One of the most heartbreaking stories in the Bible (and there are many) is that of King Solomon, third king of Israel. In 1 Kings 3:3 (NIV) we read, "Solomon showed his love for the Lord by walking according to the instructions given him by his father David, except that he offered sacrifices and burned incense on the high places." What a complicated verse that is. Solomon walked according to the instructions of God, that's the good part. But he also offered sacrifices to other gods.

Sometimes he got it right and sometimes he didn't.

Despite his faults, Solomon found favor in the Lord's eyes—so much so, in fact, that God appeared to him in a dream and gave him a great opportunity. The Lord said to him, "Ask for whatever you want me to give you" (1 Kings 3:5 NIV). That's incredible!

Can you imagine? What would you ask for? Maybe you'd wish for happiness, or a long and healthy life, or protection for your family, or maybe a better financial portfolio. Most people probably would at least consider some of those options. But Solomon didn't. Instead, he asked for wisdom.

His greatest wish was to have a wise and discerning heart. And that request pleased the Lord.

What a noble thing to ask for! Just think of the benefits of knowing God's will in every situation. You would know how to invest. Who to trust. What job to take. What battles were worth fighting. How to raise godly children. What a truly life-altering—or in Solomon's case, nation-altering—gift that would be!

Solomon asked for wisdom, and God was pleased to grant his request. "I will give you a wise and discerning heart, so that there will never have been anyone like you, nor will there ever be," the Lord told Solomon (1 Kings 3:12 NIV). With God's help, Solomon became the wisest and wealthiest man who had ever lived.

> **Reread 1 Kings 4:29, 34 (page 49). What are we told that God gave Solomon, and what happened as a result?**

God gave Solomon wisdom and insight and understanding beyond measure, and as Solomon's fame for knowledge and good decision-making spread, people from all over the world sought to learn from him. We know from what has been written about Solomon and from his own writings that his areas of wisdom included wealth, agriculture, conflict resolution, marriage, and parenting.

Under Solomon's leadership the nation of Israel flourished in many ways. But—perhaps you knew there was a "but" coming—he was not always obedient to the Lord. Remember those sacrifices he offered in obedience? Well, he was also disobedient by marrying women from other nations who turned his heart away from the Lord.

> **Reread 1 Kings 11:4 (page 49). How did Solomon's wives turn his heart away from the Lord, and how did this affect his devotion to God?**

What good is it to know God's perfect will if you don't choose to do it? For Solomon, the allure of power, women, wealth, and prestige led him astray. It sounds like Solomon fell into the same traps that Satan uses today! Instead of choosing God's will, he often chose his own; and disobedience has consequences.

Seeing things from God's perspective is wisdom. Doing those things is obedience. And knowing and doing are not always the same thing. Solomon was faithful, except when he wasn't. Those moments of exception ended up having generational consequences for his family and his nation.

Whether we realize it or not, our exceptions, also known as sins, have long-lasting implications.

Read 1 Kings 3:3 (NIV) below again and circle the word except.

Solomon showed his love for the Lᴏʀᴅ by walking according to the instructions given him by his father David, except that he offered sacrifices and burned incense on the high places.

Now read 1 Kings 11:1-13. Describe in more detail how Solomon disobeyed the Lord and what the consequences were.

In what areas of your life do you need wisdom right now?

Now, let's personalize 1 Kings 3:3. In the first blank, write your name. In the second blank, write an area where you struggle to be obedient to God.

For example: <u>Rachel</u> showed her love for the Lord by walking according to his instructions, except <u>when it came to controlling her temper</u>.

_____ showed her love for the Lord by walking according to his instructions, except

_____

_____.

We will read more of Solomon's story tomorrow, but now let's turn our attention back to the Book of James. As James led the rapidly growing but heavily persecuted first-century church, he wrote this letter to encourage and instruct the believers.

As we saw in chapter 1, James's first order of business was to alert believers that troubles are inevitable. He said we should rejoice and endure trials faithfully. Then he turned his attention to the subject of wisdom. What Solomon sought is what James encouraged the early church to seek: wisdom.

Reread James 1:5-7 (page 48). According to James, how are we to ask for wisdom?

In order to live faithfully, we need the wisdom of God. Solomon asked for wisdom, and God was quick to grant it. James encourages us to do the same. In fact, James tells us to ask without wavering. In other words, to come with a bold and confident faith before God, knowing that He can do all things. Ask God for His wisdom! It delights your heavenly Father when you want to know His heart and follow His will.

Wisdom is a top priority for the faithful believer. As Proverbs 16:16 tells us, it is better to get wisdom than gold, to get insight rather than silver! Today, friend, I encourage you to ask God for wisdom, trusting that He will give it generously!

PRAY

Natalie Grant's song "More Than Anything" has such theologically profound lyrics that include these words: "Help me want the Giver / More than the giving." You may want to pray along these lines today or perhaps listen to this song as a means of prayer.

DAY 3

SETTLE

If you listened to Natalie Grant's song "More Than Anything" yesterday, you may want to begin by listening to it again—or another song of your choice. Focus your attention on seeking God with your whole heart as you settle into a time with the One who loves you most.

FOCUS

If you are wise and understand God's ways, prove it by living an honorable life, doing good works with the humility that comes from wisdom.

(James 3:13)

I denied myself nothing my eyes desired; I refused my heart no pleasure.

(Ecclesiastes 2:10 NIV)

For the wise, like the fool, will not be long remembered.

(Ecclesiastes 2:16 NIV)

I hated all the things I had toiled for under the sun, because I must leave them to the one who comes after me. And who knows whether that person will be wise or foolish? Yet they will have control over all the fruit of my toil into which I have poured my effort and skill under the sun. This too is meaninglessness.

(Ecclesiastes 2:18 NIV)

Those who love money will never have enough. How meaningless to think that wealth brings true happiness!

(Ecclesiastes 5:10)

Seek the Kingdom of God above all else, and live righteously, and he will give you everything you need.

(Matthew 6:33)

REFLECT

Yesterday we took a look into the life of Solomon. In 1 Kings we read a good bit about him, but we can flesh out that picture by reading books that traditionally have been attributed to him: Proverbs, Song of Solomon, and Ecclesiastes.[1] Proverbs, of course, contains great wisdom and instruction. Who better to write about wisdom than the wisest person who had ever lived. Song of Solomon is a love story. But in Ecclesiastes there is a very different tone.

In this short book we see Solomon as an older man reflecting on his life. As the wisest and wealthiest man in history, he had lived a big life. His adventures and accomplishments were immense. But as Solomon reflected on his life, we see that he was filled with sorrow and regret.

> **Read Solomon's opening words in Ecclesiastes:**
>
> *"Everything is meaningless . . . completely meaningless!"*
>
> *What do people get for all their hard work under the sun? . . .*
>
> *We are never satisfied . . . we are not content.*
>
> (Ecclesiastes 1:2-3, 8)
>
> **What strikes you about Solomon's observation? Have you ever had similar thoughts? If so, write about it briefly.**

No doubt Solomon wrote this book in an attempt to spare future generations the pain and futility he had experienced.

> **In what areas of your life do you most often find yourself unsatisfied?**

On the other hand, what brings you joy and fulfillment?

Even in his wisdom, Solomon missed the most important thing in life: trusting and obeying God. His downfall came largely because he was distracted by the things of this world. When we look at verses in Ecclesiastes, we can identify four primary issues.

1. Pleasure. "I denied myself nothing my eyes desired; I refused my heart no pleasure" (Ecclesiastes 2:10 NIV).

That kind of selfish, hedonistic approach to life is sure to get anyone in trouble. Food, drink, sex, greed, entertainment, and the need for more and better is a thirst that will never be fully quenched. God wants us to enjoy life, but a life that exists in pursuit of the next feel-good moment will never be satisfied.

2. Knowledge. "For the wise, like the fool, will not be long remembered" (Ecclesiastes 2:16 NIV).

Solomon enjoyed the pursuit of knowledge as well as pleasure. He studied a vast array of subjects and became the scholar among scholars of his time. His quest to know about things overtook his quest to know the Creator of those things.

3. Achievement. "I hated all the things I had toiled for under the sun, because I must leave them to the one who comes after me. And who knows whether that person will be wise or foolish? Yet they will have control over all the fruit of my toil into which I have poured my effort and skill under the sun. This too is meaninglessness" (Ecclesiastes 2:18 NIV).

Solomon worked hard in his lifetime. He was a master builder, a warrior, a horseman, and a savvy businessman—not to mention, he was the king of a powerful nation. Yet, as he reflected on his life, he realized that in the big picture none of it mattered, because none of it would last forever.

4. Wealth. "Those who love money will never have enough. How meaningless to think that wealth brings true happiness!" (Ecclesiastes 5:10).

Money and possessions can easily become too great a priority in the life of a believer. Solomon fell victim to this trap.

> **In what ways do these four things that distracted Solomon from God serve as distractions in your own life? What else distracts you from following Christ? Make a few notes below.**
>
> **Pleasure:**
>
>
>
> **Knowledge:**
>
>
>
> **Achievement:**
>
>
>
> **Wealth:**
>
>
>
> **Other:**
>
>
>
> **What can you do to prioritize your relationship with Jesus on a daily basis?**

Even in his wisdom, Solomon missed the most important thing in life: trusting and obeying God.

If Ecclesiastes ended with these laments, it would be a depressing message for sure. But in the last verses of Ecclesiastes, Solomon gets to his final analysis.

Read Ecclesiastes 12:13-14 and write Solomon's final conclusion below:

In other words, Solomon is saying, "I've had it all and done it all, but what I have learned is that nothing matters without a relationship with God." It took the wisest man who ever lived a lifetime to learn what matters most. He wasn't fulfilled with knowledge, money, achievement, or pleasure. What he came to understand was that true wisdom is knowing and obeying God.

Now, back to James. He knew that his friends and fellow believers would be tempted in their difficult circumstances to look for purpose, comfort, and meaning in things other than a relationship with God. It would have been easy for them to become distracted by persecution and focus on their problems instead of their faith. Therefore, he pleaded with them to seek wisdom and live according to it, not giving into temptation but living for the One who loved them most. His words still ring true. If we are wise and understand God's ways, we prove it by living honorable lives, doing good works with the humility that comes from wisdom.

Reread James 3:13 (page 54) and rewrite it below in your own words:

What is the evidence of a truly wise person?

> **If we are wise and understand God's ways, we prove it by living honorable lives, doing good works with the humility that comes from wisdom.**

The truly wise life is not marked by knowledge but by living according to God's word. The truly wise person may, in fact, be simple by the world's standards. Others may not view them as successful, but in the end, it is only God's view that will matter.

As I reflect on Solomon's life, I can't help thinking of a high school friend who recently took his own life. The news of his death was a shock to all who knew and loved him. He was delightful. Professionally, he was a success. He was smart and creative, and when I was around him, I laughed—a lot. It was the good kind of laughing, too. The kind that left my cheeks stained with tears. He was usually the life of the party and always made me feel loved.

Why would he end his life? He had so many friends. What happened? Apparently, his life was lacking something, and I wonder if that something was eternal hope. Did he know Jesus? I mean really know Him. Because without the eternal hope of Christ, where do people find meaning to go on when life is hard? When the success fades and the relationships are rocky, where do they turn?

> **Is there anything your life is lacking right now? How does the eternal hope of Christ give you meaning even when life is hard?**

Without Jesus, I agree with Solomon, it must all be so meaningless. That's why we need a Savior. And we need His wisdom and eternal hope to live this life well.

So then, what do we learn from Solomon and James? It can be summed up in the words of Jesus himself.

Draw a line beneath what we are to do and draw two lines beneath what God will do in response.

"Seek the Kingdom of God above all else, and live righteously, and he will give you everything you need."

(Matthew 6:33)

Throughout your day, focus on what matters most: Jesus. Focus on Him. Share Him. Love Him. This will lead you into wisdom. This will bring you and others eternal hope.

PRAY

Lord Jesus, help me to seek You first in all things. Forgive me when I become distracted. Help me not to be led into temptation but to live for You and You only. Today I give You myself anew. I love You, Lord. Amen.

DAY 4

SETTLE

As you turn aside from the day's demands, consider how God has been present in your life. Thank Him for His presence and love today.

FOCUS

But the wisdom from above is first pure, then peaceable, gentle, open to reason, full of mercy and good fruits, impartial and sincere.

(James 3:17 ESV)

Wisdom is the most important thing. So get wisdom.
If it costs everything you have, get understanding.
Believe in the value of wisdom, and it will make you great.
Use it, and it will bring honor to you.

(Proverbs 4:7-8 ICB)

The way of a fool is right in his own eyes,
but a wise man listens to advice.

(Proverbs 12:15 ESV)

Whoever trusts in his own mind is a fool,
but he who walks in wisdom will be delivered.

(Proverbs 28:26 ESV)

Then you will call on me and come and pray to me, and I will listen to you. You will seek me and find me when you seek me with all your heart.

(Jeremiah 29:12-13 NIV)

REFLECT

Probably the most often asked question I've had over my years of ministry is this: How can I know God's will for my life? It's a great question. It's important. If you're like me, the idea of being busy your entire life only to find in the end that you were busy with the wrong things would be devastating. My guess is that you have asked this many times in your life: Lord, what is your will for my life?

In general terms, you can know God's will. It is God's will for you to know Him, to love and obey Him, and to share Him with others. That's the simple version. You won't go wrong with these three goals:

1. Know God personally.
2. Love and obey him.
3. Share him with others.

That's the big picture for all of us. But often when we're asking the question of our purpose, we're looking for more specific answers. We want to know whom we should marry, what career path to take, whether or not to have children, how to invest, and the list goes on. How do we go about making wise decisions in our day-to-day lives?

My guess is if you've been a believer for a while, you pray about things and listen, and then you get down to the business of making a logical decision. You weigh out the pros and cons and study the list and then make the most rational, intelligent choice. The problem is, sometimes the logical decision is not the wisest one, or the one God is calling you to make.

When I was five months pregnant with my son, my husband announced that he thought we should quit our jobs, which we loved, and move to a new area to start a church for unchurched people. He said, "We'll build a steakhouse for vegetarians. A church for people who don't know they need a church. A family of God for people who aren't yet in the family." (Now, if you're a vegetarian, more power to you! Jim happens to love steak, so I understood what he meant.)

Now, that sounds noble. And, I had no doubt that Jim was sincere. But I had a three-year-old, a baby on the way, and a steady paycheck. It sounded like a terrible life plan to me. What was he thinking? This made no sense. Quit our jobs and move to a place we don't know, where there is no land available, no people, no one asking for another church, and no long-term source of income? It seemed like a hard pass to me.

But I love my husband, and I wanted to see his dreams come to life. So we prayed. A lot. But our situation didn't change. Well, it changed a little; I

Sometimes the logical decision is not the wisest one, or the one God is calling you to make.

was no longer pregnant. Now I had a newborn. But the rest of it was still scary and made no sense.

I began to dwell on Scriptures like Proverbs 28:26 (ESV), "Whoever trusts in his own mind is a fool, but he who walks in wisdom will be delivered." Eventually, I surrendered my will to God's and said, "Okay, I want to walk in your wisdom. I want to support my husband. But Lord, this is scary. Tell us clearly what to do, please!"

At that point, Jim and I began to really seek God's will for our little family. In doing that, we discovered four steps to help us tune into God's spirit and discover His will. As you seek God's wisdom, I encourage you to try these four steps as well.

Pray

Get on your knees! Not for a few minutes or a day or two. Go to God over an extended period of time and simply seek Him. There is no magic formula for how you pray; just pour your heart out to your heavenly Father and then wait in silence to hear from Him.

Meditate on the Scriptures in the margin. What stands out and catches your attention? Write your thoughts in the space below.

1 Peter 3:12

For the eyes of the Lord are on the righteous and his ears are attentive to their prayer.
(1 Peter 3:12 NIV)

Jeremiah 29:12-13

Then you will call on me and come and pray to me, and I will listen to you. You will seek me and find me when you seek me with all your heart.
(Jeremiah 29:12-13 NIV)

Is prayer your first reaction or last resort when faced with a decision? What in your approach to prayer needs to change in order for you to seek God with all your heart?

Study God's Word

Dig into Scripture to discover what God has already said concerning your situation. One of the ways to find His will is to know His word.

I pondered the direction of my life, and I turned to follow your laws.
    (Psalm 119:59)

Meditate on the Scriptures in the margin. What stands out and catches your attention? Write your thoughts in the space below.

Psalm 119:59

Your word is a lamp to my feet
  and a light to my path.
    (Psalm 119:105 ESV)

Psalm 119:105

Circle the choice below that best describes your current Bible study routine:

Daily   **Seasonally**   **Randomly**

Rarely   **Can't find my Bible, Jen**

Seek Godly Counsel

Go to the most mature believers you know and seek their advice. Invite them to pray with you and offer their best counsel for your situation.

Without counsel plans fail, but with many advisers they succeed.
    (Proverbs 15:22 ESV)

Meditate on the Scriptures in the margin. What stands out and catches your attention? Write your thoughts in the space below.

Proverbs 15:22

The way of a fool is right in his own eyes, but a wise man listens to advice.
    (Proverbs 12:15 ESV)

Proverbs 12:15

Who are your go-to people when needing advice? Are they mature believers?

Wait for God's peace

There truly is a peace that passes all human understanding that can settle upon those who seek God's perfect will. It may not make sense to others, but when God speaks and you know it is Him, you have the confidence to follow Him. James refers to this peace in 3:17 when he describes God's wisdom as peaceable, gentle, open to reason, full of mercy and good fruits, impartial and sincere. Imagine all the ways you would benefit from this kind of wisdom. James wanted the believers of the early church to know and seek wisdom from God that would yield them the power of God's peace and presence in their difficult situation.

Meditate on the Scriptures in the margin. What stands out and catches your attention? Write your thoughts in the space below.

Philippians 4:7

James 3:17

The peace of God, which surpasses all understanding, will guard your hearts and minds through Christ Jesus.
    (Philippians 4:7 NKJV)

But the wisdom from above is first pure, then peaceable, gentle, open to reason, full of mercy and good fruits, impartial and sincere.
    (James 3:17 ESV)

What does it look like in your life for you to dwell in God's peace?

After a season of going through the first three steps, we came to what I would call a nervous peace. Nervous because it was new, scary, and big. But it was peace because we knew God was in it. It was a big task starting this church for those who don't know they need a church, but we felt God's leading. What we needed now was His wisdom in how to go about things. And it wasn't a one-time request. It became a state of living. We learned to live in a state of seeking God's wisdom and will. We were in over our heads and needed Him every step of the way. Wisdom became our goal—staying close to Jesus so that we didn't miss a step. Proverbs 4:7-8 (ICB) tells us, "Wisdom is the most important thing. So get wisdom. If it costs everything you have, get understanding."

The good news is it turned out well. Over forty-two hundred people have chosen to give their lives to Christ through this church that we've been a part of, and we know it's all God's doing!

As we've discovered this week, wisdom is seeing our circumstances from God's perspective and discerning how He would choose for us to live. Sometimes there's not one right answer but several options that would be pleasing to God, and these steps can help us in that discernment process. Wisdom is the most important thing. So, as you go out today, make wisdom your goal, and the often-asked question about God's will for your life will come into focus. As we discern God's will, we discover how best to live each and every day.

PRAY

God, You tell us to pray and ask for wisdom, so again today I ask: would You give me a wise and discerning mind to know Your will and Your way? (Take time to just sit quietly and listen for God to speak to your heart.) Amen.

DAY 5

SETTLE

Stand up and take a few deep breaths to calm your spirit. Then use this week's memory verse (James 1:5) as a request to the Lord today. Ask Him to give you wisdom and new insight during this concentrated time you will spend with Him.

FOCUS

Consider it pure joy, my brothers and sisters, whenever you face trials of many kinds, because you know that the testing of your faith produces perseverance. Let perseverance finish its work so that you may be mature and complete, not lacking anything. If any of you lacks wisdom, you should ask God, who gives generously to all without finding fault, and it will be given to you. But when you ask, you must believe and not doubt, because the one who doubts is like a wave of the sea, blown and tossed by the wind. That person should not expect to receive anything from the Lord. Such a person is double-minded and unstable in all they do.

(James 1:2-8 NIV)

When pride comes, then comes disgrace,
but with humility comes wisdom.
(Proverbs 11:2 NIV)

You will seek me and find me when you seek me with all your heart.
(Jeremiah 29:13 NIV)

REFLECT

For a city girl, learning to drive can be a challenge. My husband, a country boy, learned to drive trucks and tractors in wide-open spaces at a young age. As a result, when it came time to get his license, he was well seasoned behind the wheel. But when you grow up in the city, empty parking lots are about the best you get for practicing in. My parents would take me out in those parking lots with no other traffic and wide spaces to turn, and I did pretty well. My conclusion at the age of fifteen, with all the wisdom I had acquired from my parking lot adventures, was that I am a great driver.

So, when my mom and I headed into Atlanta one day, I said, "I've got this. I'll drive." I did pretty well until a torrential storm blew up. I mean it was ugly. Mom got tense. I was nervous. We both knew I was in over my head, but the rain was so heavy that pulling over would have been dangerous. So, we trudged along, but it was a scary situation. As soon as it was safe to do so, I parked and we switched places. This was too much; I needed help. I started out confident, but when things got really hard, we both knew that more skill was needed behind the wheel.

When have you felt in over your head?

What kind of help did you need?

Every time you face a difficulty in life you have an opportunity to discover where your faith is lacking. You also have an opportunity for growth. As we saw last week, through our difficulties our faith has the opportunity to persevere and mature.

Reread James 1:2-4 once again (page 67). According to James, why are we to consider difficulties an opportunity for growth?

Many times over the years, Jim and I have received news that someone in our church family is experiencing pain. That pain could be from the loss of a loved one, such as a child or a spouse. It might be the discovery of infidelity or of job loss. Or it might be a dreaded medical diagnosis. As we have sat with friends during those times, we have observed that people of faith handle these crises in very different ways. In most cases, we come onto the scene knowing what to expect—devastating sadness, perhaps anger, even a numb sense of disbelief.

But every now and then, we arrive to find incredible peace in the storm. Sadness is present but there is also a clear sense of hope. I remember once in an especially difficult situation with the death of a child, the parents quoted Scripture to us and assured us that God was in control and would bring something beautiful out of this pain. They were comforting us as we grieved with them!

Mature faith endures, hopes, trusts, and finds peace in the darkest moments.

At first, I thought they were in shock or denial. But I realized over the coming months they were truly relying on God in all things. They had a deep faith that had grown over many years. They had faced difficulties before and had learned to solely rely on Christ. They knew that they could not handle this pain without letting God have control. That spiritual maturity was paying off in this most painful season. Jesus was their hope in life and in death, and their faith was unwavering.

This family taught me that mature faith endures, hopes, trusts, and finds peace in the darkest moments. They lived out what James is teaching us: Face the trials of your life with joy, because through those troubles God perfects your faith and grows you into a person of maturity, complete with the mind and heart of Christ.

The maturity James is talking about rarely occurs in a one-time event; it's a process over time. So, as we've seen this week, he instructs us what to do when faith falls short during times of difficulty:

If any of you lacks wisdom, you should ask God, who gives generously to all without finding fault, and it will be given to you.

(James 1:5 NIV)

Take a moment to paraphrase James 1:2-8 in your own words:

Here's my paraphrase of James's instructions:

> When hard times come into your life, you can be excited about what will result from those difficulties. Because, as you are faithful in times of testing, it will cause your faith to grow and you will become strong, mature, brave, and true for Jesus. Eventually, you will be left with no deficiencies in your faith. But if you find that your faith falls short, and it will, then pray for wisdom. Ask God for His help and He will gladly give you the help you need as your faith matures.

James is realistic in his instruction and encouragement. He is aware that perfection, or spiritual maturity, comes from perseverance. But this takes time. As a runner gains endurance by putting in mile after mile, so a Christian builds endurance by facing one difficulty after another with faith and spiritual maturity.

Just as I needed my mom's driving experience and skill in that storm in Atlanta, there are times, especially when our faith is not yet fully mature, that we need to cry out to God for His help and wisdom to navigate the storms of our life, trusting that He will answer us. However, all too often God is a last resort for us instead of a first response in times of struggle. We want to solve our problems ourselves.

In that storm, when the first raindrops began to sprinkle, I assured my mom that I could handle driving in the rain. What I didn't realize was how quickly that sprinkle would turn into a downpour. In hindsight, the wiser move would have been to stop at the first sign of the storm and surrender the wheel. I simply didn't have enough experience as a driver to handle what was in front of me; I needed my mom to take over. I needed to surrender the wheel.

When you face struggles, what is typically your first response?

When recently have you cried out to God and "surrendered the wheel"? What happened?

If you're like me, when things get hard, I try harder. I work the problem. I may ask for advice or study best practices. But all too often, and I'm embarrassed to admit this, I want to handle things myself. The problem is that without God, I am always found lacking. I'm not smart enough, skilled enough, or wise enough to face all this life can throw at me. Can you relate?

Reread Proverbs 11:2 (page 67). How is this verse a warning? What can hinder our wisdom?

What we desperately need is God's wisdom. This week our attention has been focused on seeking wisdom in all that we do. Seeing things from God's perspective and moving according to His will is true wisdom.

Friends, I want you to do what both Proverbs and James tell us to do: seek wisdom! It is the most important thing. And here is the awesome news: God wants to give you His insight. In fact, as James says, He's glad to do it!

PRAY

Meditate on Jeremiah 29:13. Thank God for His presence in your life. Pray and ask Him to give you wisdom in whatever you are facing today. Thank Him, in advance, that as you seek Him you will find Him.

You will seek me and find me when you seek me with all your heart.

(Jeremiah 29:13 NIV)

Video Viewer Guide: WEEK 2

Wisdom

Having Heavenly Perspective on Earthly Issues

If any of you lacks wisdom, you should ask God, who gives generously to all without finding fault, and it will be given to you.

(James 1:5)

It's possible to _____ _____ as a believer without _____ ____ as a believer.

Sin _____ us from God.

_____ is a mark of Christian maturity.

Simple steps to get started:

1.   We intentionally _____ _____ to God.

2.   We must ____ what God says.

Week 3

ACTION

Living a Life Where Actions Match Faith

Memory Verse

Do not merely listen to the word, and so deceive yourselves. Do what it says.

(James 1:22 NIV)

DAY 1

SETTLE

Reread and then mediate on this week's memory verse, James 1:22 (page 74). Read it several times, placing emphasis on different words like this:

Do not MERELY listen to the word, and so deceive yourselves. Do what it says.
Do not merely listen to the word, and so DECEIVE yourselves. Do what it says.
Do NOT merely listen to the word, and so deceive yourselves. Do what it says.
Do not merely LISTEN to the word, and so deceive yourselves. Do what is says.
Do not merely listen to the word, and so deceive yourselves. DO what it says.

FOCUS

From James, a slave of God and of the Lord Jesus Christ. To the twelve tribes who are scattered outside the land of Israel. Greetings!

(James 1:1 CEB)

What good is it, dear brothers and sisters, if you say you have faith but don't show it by your actions? Can that kind of faith save anyone? Suppose you see a brother or sister who has no food or clothing, and you say, "Good-bye and have a good day; stay warm and eat well"—but then you don't give that person any food or clothing. What good does that do?

So you see, faith by itself isn't enough. Unless it produces good deeds, it is dead and useless.

Now someone may argue, "Some people have faith; others have good deeds." But I say, "How can you show me your faith if you don't have good deeds? I will show you my faith by my good deeds."

You say you have faith, for you believe that there is one God. Good for you! Even the demons believe this, and they tremble in terror. How foolish! Can't you see that faith without good deeds is useless?

(James 2:14-20)

Without faith it is impossible to please God, because anyone who comes to him must believe that he exists and that he rewards those who earnestly seek him.

(Hebrews 11:6 NIV)

REFLECT

Having spent almost forty years in ministry, let me clue you in on a little secret among many church leaders I know. We have a pet peeve. It's pretty common, actually. It's when Christians tell us that they're "praying about" whether or not to get involved in ministry.

Listen, there are a lot of things in life you need to pray about. Whom to marry, which job to take, whether or not to have children, and which home to buy—all are things for which you should spend time in prayer. But whether or not you serve in ministry is not one of them. You don't have to waste your time praying on that one because the answer is "Yes, serve." "Yes, get involved." "Yes, make a difference." "Yes, find your place in the family of God and serve with all your heart." If you try a ministry and it's not for you, then try another one. But don't let anything or anyone, even yourself, keep you from living into God's plan for you.

Now, I may have lost some of you in the last paragraph. But stay with me. If you're like me, when something steps on your toes, you immediately go on the defensive. That posture of defense leads us to explain, rationalize, make our excuses, or perhaps just tune out altogether. But let's not do that because, as we'll see in this week's lessons in James, real faith is backed up by action.

When have you seen someone's faith in action and thought it a powerful testimony?

How do you put your faith into action on a weekly basis? (For example, taking meals to the sick, volunteering at church or in the community, leading a Bible study, refusing to gossip, caring for the poor, visiting shut-ins and widows, and so forth.)

What keeps you from putting your faith into actions on a regular basis?

I hope you've read through the entire Book of James now. If not, you may want to do that today. It is a short, practical, and easy-to-read letter. In fact, it reads more like a parent giving life instructions to a dearly loved child than a theologian instructing disciples.

If we circle back to the very beginning of the letter, we see that James identifies himself with this description: "James, a servant of God and the Lord Jesus Christ" (James 1:1 NIV). In many translations, the word used for servant is actually *slave*. There is no doubt James is establishing that he is fully committed to the Lord he serves. From his first words, he wants his readers to know that his life, as well as every believer's life, must be defined by servitude. We are to be servants, not just disciples, of God.

Think about the life of a servant, or to be more extreme, a slave. Their life ceases to be their own. What they do, and how and when they do it, is at the discretion of the one they serve. Servanthood is a primary theme of this letter.

James emphasizes that those who call themselves followers of Christ must submit in every way to the Lordship of Jesus. He highlights day by day trademarks of a true believer, such as practicing clean speech, wisdom, humility, and endurance; caring for orphans and widows; embracing holiness; and developing an active prayer life. As we saw last week, it reads very much like a New Testament version of Proverbs. There is wisdom for daily living in almost every verse. And as James offers this instruction, he doesn't hold back. In the fashion of his half-brother, Jesus, he calls out hypocrites and allows for no excuses when it comes to living out what we believe. As this week's memory verse commands, we must do what God's Word tells us, and not be deceived by being hearers only.

Write James 1:22 below:

How does the Kingdom suffer when we do not live out our faith in practical ways?

> More than any other book of the New Testament, James emphasizes the absolute necessity for a believer's actions to match his or her beliefs.

More than any other book of the New Testament, James emphasizes the absolute necessity for a believer's actions to match his or her beliefs. When we get this wrong—when we say we follow Christ but don't live in Christlike ways—the ramifications affect not only us but also those who are watching our testimony. And people are always watching.

In Hebrews 11:6 (NIV) we read, "Without faith it is impossible to please God, because anyone who comes to him must believe that he exists and that he rewards those who earnestly seek him." That's the first step—believing, or having faith. But James takes it further: Real faith is moved to action. As he would say, a faith that doesn't have deeds is useless. Or worse, as in the case of Gandhi, it actually does harm to the faith journey of others.

Can you recall a time when you were affected by the lack of love in action on the part of other believers? If so, write about it briefly below.

Look again at James 1:22 (that you wrote on the previous page) and indicate below who is deceived by faith without deeds.

It's not *others* we are deceiving with a faith that has no fruit. They can see our actions clearly. It's not *God* who is confused. Surely, He knows us best of all. The danger is that *we* are the ones deceived. *We* are the ones lulled into a false sense of spiritual security when our faith does not produce fruit. James says that we should not merely listen to the word of God and deceive *ourselves*.

A profession of faith, even a sincere one, is not enough to live a vital life in Christ. The life that is devoted to Jesus reveals itself through its fruit—through action.

Reread James 2:14-20 (page 75). Take a moment to meditate on verse 16. How do these words speak to you?

How does James describe a faith without action in verse 17?

James uses dramatic language here when he describes a faith without action as dead. What a tragedy!

So, as we begin this week, I've got a challenge for you: put your faith into action in a new way. Either alone or with your Bible study group, call your pastor and ask, "What most needs to be done in the church?" Then go do it. Do the toilets need scrubbing? Do it. Toys need cleaning? Do it. People need food? Organize a casserole drive and start cooking. No excuses. Ask what the needs are and then get busy meeting them.

It's a way to bless your church and put your faith into action. It's a way to thrive as a Christian. It may not be where you're called to serve long-term, and that's okay. But it will give you a chance to put your faith into action in a new way.

PRAY

Lord, here I am. How can we partner together this week?

Go ahead and call your pastor, or a ministry leader, and put your faith into action.

DAY 2

SETTLE

Begin by listening to a favorite song that brings you peace. Ask the Lord to help you receive from His Word and put this message into action this week.

FOCUS

Do not merely listen to the word, and so deceive yourselves. Do what it says. Anyone who listens to the word but does not do what it says is like someone who looks at his face in a mirror and, after looking at himself, goes away and immediately forgets what he looks like. But whoever looks intently into the perfect law that gives freedom, and continues in it—not forgetting what they have heard, but doing it—they will be blessed in what they do.

(James 1:22-25 NIV)

A faith that does not do things is a dead faith.

(James 2:17 NLV)

"Teacher, which is the greatest commandment in the Law?"

Jesus replied: "'Love the Lord your God with all your heart and with all your soul and with all your mind.' This is the first and greatest commandment. And the second is like it: 'Love your neighbor as yourself.' All the Law and the Prophets hang on these two commandments."

(Matthew 22:36-40 NIV)

REFLECT

When I was pregnant with my daughter, Alyssa, I would walk every morning at a local mall. My husband and I were in seminary and couldn't afford a gym membership. So, walking at the mall, which was large and air-conditioned, was a great solution. After a few weeks in my new work-out setting, I made friends with my fellow mall walkers. We varied in age from early twenties to late eighties. We were very different people, and it was a joy to meet up each morning. We had the fast walkers, the casual walkers, the slow walkers, and the ones who said they were there to walk but usually just drank coffee. We were an odd but delightful group.

I developed two friendships that became particularly close during that time. First, there was Joe, an elderly widower, who could hang with the fast walkers. And Cara, a hard-working single mom who struggled to make ends meet. Monday through Friday I would leave home early and drive the thirty minutes toward my job in order to get to the mall for a quick two miles with Joe, Cara, and the rest of the crew.

They all watched, and commented, as my belly grew over the months. Toward the end of my pregnancy, I went from the fast-walking crowd to the casual-walking group. As I slowed down, Cara slowed down with me. She stayed right by my side every morning. Joe, on the other hand, was still friendly but wasn't about to slow down. He was chasing the widows in the fast-walking crowd. Good for you, Joe!

Then one day, about eight months into my pregnancy, I had a tough morning. I became lightheaded on my second lap and had to sit for a while. Cara sat with me. We quickly realized something wasn't quite right. I asked Cara to call my husband so he could leave class and come get me. She just stared at me and said, "Is that how it works in your church? Because in my church, when someone is in need, we stop what we're doing and we help. Girl, you need help. I'm driving you home. Your husband can come get the car. Now, where do you live?"

Now, that was really sweet, but I lived thirty minutes out, and for her to take me home would mean her missing a shift at work. My first instinct was that there was no way I was letting her lose some of her paycheck on my account.

But she insisted, "This is what Christians do, Jen. We show up. We put our faith into action. It's who we are. It's what we do. Even when it's hard. Now, let's get you home."

And then she did. She got me home, put me in bed, and waited until Jim got there. Friends, I'm teary as I write this. It was love in action. She was living out her faith, and I was the beneficiary that day. "A faith that does not do things is a dead faith" (James 2:17 NLV).

Jim and I didn't have much materially at the time, but Cara had less. When I needed someone, she put her needs aside and took care of me. Even when it was hard. Even when it cost her. She taught me a lot about what it means to be a Christian that day. (Everything turned out fine with my pregnancy, by the way, just a little pre-labor pain).

Cara was a great example for me of doing more than listening to God's word. She immediately went into action. For her, the sermon on Sunday and her life on Monday ran parallel. Unfortunately, at times we know more than we are doing. James warns against this. For us to fully live into our potential as God's girls, we must show up, allow ourselves to be inconvenienced, and do what God's word instructs us to do: care for the sick, help the poor, love the difficult, be patient with everyone, and the list goes on.

When has someone shown up for you?

Paraphrase this week's memory verse, James 1:22, in your own words below:

Who needs you to show up for them right now?

The title of this study is "Thrive." For your faith to really do that will require action. You will have to move beyond belief, beyond words, and beyond excuses to become active in living out the Great Commandment and Great Commission. So, let's remind ourselves what those two important passages are all about.

Great Commandment:

"Teacher, which is the greatest commandment in the Law?"

Jesus replied: "'Love the Lord your God with all your heart and with all your soul and with all your mind.' This is the first and greatest commandment. And the second is like it: 'Love your neighbor as yourself.' All the Law and the Prophets hang on these two commandments."

(Matthew 22:36-40 NIV)

What is the two-part Great Commandment?

1.

2.

Great Commission:

Then the eleven disciples went to Galilee, to the mountain where Jesus had told them to go. When they saw him, they worshiped him; but some doubted. Then Jesus came to them and said, "All authority in heaven and on earth has been given to me. Therefore go and make disciples of all nations, baptizing them in the name of the Father and of the Son and of the Holy Spirit, and teaching them to obey everything I have commanded you. And surely I am with you always, to the very end of the age."

(Matthew 28:16-20 NIV)

What three instructions do we find in verses 19 and 20?

1.

2.

3.

All Scripture is certainly important and inspired by God, but these two passages are among the cornerstones of the entire Christian faith. Putting these into practice is essential if you want to live in a way that pleases God. If we were to simplify these classic Scripture, we might say this:

- Love God first and foremost.
- Go out of your way to love other people.
- Share Christ in ways that lead others to Him.

Today, let's focus on the Great Commandment. This passage occurs at a time when Jesus is being challenged by church leaders. In fact, my translation actually says Jesus is being tested by a teacher with the question, "Which is the greatest commandment in the Law?" (It's never a good idea to test Jesus.) In response, Jesus goes straight to the bottom line: love God and love others. That's it—it's all about love.

Yesterday I shared a pet peeve. Well, here's another (I really don't have that many; they're just really applicable this week). It's when people ask for the deep, hard teachings of the faith. I guess when people ask this question, they are wanting a Greek translation or some church history thrown into the mix. But friends, there is no deeper teaching than this: love God and love others. It sounds simple, but again, simple isn't always easy.

> **You know from experience that loving God and loving others isn't always easy. Give a recent example of when acting in love wasn't easy.**

What was the outcome of that experience? What kind of effect did putting your faith into action through love have?

Loving God completely, making Him the first priority of your life, is the deep stuff. That's the hard, faithful, committed act of a believer. Taking that faith and putting it into action to benefit others is the advanced work of the Christ follower.

Friends, if you want your faith to thrive, then it will involve action. It will be marked by a life that is inconvenienced, that spends money and time on others, that cares for those who in no way can repay you. It is a faith that misses a shift at work to take care your very pregnant walking buddy. It is a faith that lives out the Great Commandment. Because, as Jesus said, loving God and loving others is the most important thing.

PRAY

Jesus, help me see people the way You see them. Let my heart break for what breaks Your heart. I want to be available to love and help people even when I'm inconvenienced. Change me, mold me, make me who You want me to be. I love You, Lord. Amen.

DAY 3

SETTLE

Listen to "Send Me" by Jen Johnson as you quiet your heart before the Lord today.

FOCUS

Do not merely listen to the word, and so deceive yourselves. Do what it says. Anyone who listens to the word but does not do what it says is like someone who looks at his face in a mirror and, after looking at himself, goes away and immediately forgets what he looks like. But whoever looks intently into the perfect law that gives freedom, and continues in it—not forgetting what they have heard, but doing it—they will be blessed in what they do.

(James 1:22-25 NIV)

And I heard the voice of the Lord saying, "Whom shall I send, and who will go for us?" Then I said, "Here I am! Send me."

(Isaiah 6:8 ESV)

Then the eleven disciples went to Galilee, to the mountain where Jesus had told them to go. When they saw him, they worshiped him; but some doubted. Then Jesus came to them and said, "All authority in heaven and on earth has been given to me. Therefore go and make disciples of all nations, baptizing them in the name of the Father and of the Son and of the Holy Spirit, and teaching them to obey everything I have commanded you. And surely I am with you always, to the very end of the age."

(Matthew 28:16-20 NIV)

REFLECT

On Thursday mornings you will often find me leading a ladies Bible study in my church. We usually get everyone talking with an opening question. But it's not your typical "What's your favorite movie?" kind of question. It's more like "How is it with your soul?" or "Where are you struggling in your faith?" Recently, the question was "How did you come to know Jesus personally?"

It was one of the most eye-opening moments of my ministry. The responses ranged from "I was a little girl in vacation Bible school" to "I don't understand the question." Some of these friends have been in my life for decades, yet I was surprised to hear that it was only recently that many of them had moved from church attender to Christ follower. I was even more surprised to realize that a few of them still did not have a personal relationship with Jesus.

So, I began to pray for them privately. I prayed for the group as a whole, but for a few of them, the prayers became very specific. I didn't want to run them off, but I felt we had to find a way to share the gospel that would change their eternal trajectory.

It intrigued me that they were so faithful in church, even in Bible study, but didn't know Jesus. Why did they continue to come? Were they there for the friendships, the snacks? So, before we broke for the summer, I told the group that I had been praying for them. It was a bold moment. I told them that for some of them I was praying they would begin to use their talents and abilities to serve others. For others, I had been praying they would begin to understand their spiritual gifting so that God could use them in more powerful ways. For some, the prayer was for healing, physically and emotionally. But for two of them, I was praying that they would come to know Jesus as their personal Savior.

At the end of our group, one of the ladies, a sharp, feisty seventy-five-year-old gal, approached me and said, "I'm one of the two, right?" I just nodded. She said, "I know. But Jen, you have to understand all the people who should have loved me in my life, didn't—not my mom, dad, or husband(s). Why would God be different?" We talked a moment. She cried. I hugged her and reassured her that when she was ready, so was God. And so was I. I told her I'd love to pray with her when she was ready to receive Jesus. She left saying she needed time to think.

An hour later, Jim came into my office and said, "Three of the ladies from your group are still in the parking lot. They're praying together, I think." I went and watched from a distance as she and two precious friends prayed with her to receive Jesus. I'm not sure what happened in the one-hundred-yard journey from our talk to the parking lot, but she was ready. And they were there for her.

She told me later, "I'll never need a diet again. In that moment, in that parking lot, I lost sixty pounds and sixty years of baggage. I'm happy. I'm free."

I share that story with you because it's fresh on my heart, but also because I'm so thankful for the two ladies who prayed with her in the parking lot. One has a special needs child; the other is a mom of six. They both had places to be, but they knew nowhere was more important than right where they were, in a parking lot praying with their friend.

Whom do you need to thank for investing in your life? How did they pour into you?

How did you come to personally know Jesus? (And if, like some of the women in my Bible study group, you don't understand the question, contact me and we'll talk: jen@harvestchurch4u.org.)

For whom do you need to be praying to have a personal, saving relationship with Jesus?

Yesterday, we focused on the Great Commandment, loving God and loving others. We spent time focusing on James's instruction to not merely listen to God's word but also do what it says. Today, as we continue to focus on putting our faith into action, we are digging into the Great Commission.

Let me set the stage for this famous passage. Jesus had taught, assembled the Twelve, and performed miracles. He had endured false trials, beatings, and death on a cross. Three days later He was resurrected and spent time sharing the hope of eternal life. But now, the time had come for Him to ascend to heaven. This was an important moment.

Reread Matthew 28:36-40 (page 87). What did the Son of God say in his final moments with his team? Summarize Jesus's words below:

Jesus said, "Go!" He sent them forth. He commissioned them to go and make disciples. This was his final instruction.

Look at these famous quotes about disciple-making from great pastors and theologians:

God forbid that I should travel with anybody a quarter of an hour without speaking of Christ to them.

—George Whitefield[1]

Our faith becomes stronger as we express it; a growing faith is a sharing faith.

—Billy Graham[2]

How do these quotes speak to you?

Does making disciples sound like a daunting assignment? It does for many people. But let's make it simple. Do what was done for my friend in the parking lot.

1. Develop real friendships with those who are far from God.
2. Pray for them to come into a personal relationship with Jesus.
3. Share your faith when the time is right.

There is not a one-size-fits-all method to sharing your faith. It comes down to loving God so much that your heart begins to break for those who don't yet know Him. Then be ready to lean in. Lean in to share your own faith. Lean in to ask how you can pray for them. Lean in and ask them what their relationship with God is like. Focus on loving them and building a solid friendship, and the rest will follow. But be intentional. Get serious about leading people to Christ.

Putting your faith into action can take many forms. Feeding the hungry, caring for the hurting, and serving in your churches' ministries are a few possibilities. But nothing will have longer-term effects than leading someone into a relationship with Jesus. Friends, a Christian who is thriving is about the business of making disciples. So, let's do that. Let's put our faith into action and go and share Jesus!

> **There is not a one-size-fits-all method to sharing your faith.**

PRAY

God, thank You for loving me. Thank You for trusting me with the Great Commission. Help me to see those who need to know You and be available to share my faith in ways that will help them come to know You personally. As the song I listened to today says, "Here I am Lord, send Me." I will go. Amen.

DAY 4

SETTLE

Today, you may want to go outside for your devotion (weather permitting). Close your eyes and listen for a few minutes. Take in all the sounds around you—birds singing, wind rustling in the trees, water running, kids playing, traffic whizzing by. Notice what you may usually miss. As you turn your attention to Jesus, ask Him to help you hear His voice in ways you have missed before. Listen for Him to speak to you in new and amazing ways about who you are, those in need, who He is, and how He is leading you in this moment.

FOCUS

What good is it, my brothers and sisters, if someone claims to have faith but has no deeds? Can such faith save them? Suppose a brother or a sister is without clothes and daily food. If one of you says to them, "Go in peace; keep warm and well fed," but does nothing about their physical needs, what good is it? In the same way, faith by itself, if it is not accompanied by action, is dead.

But someone will say, "You have faith; I have deeds."

Show me your faith without deeds, and I will show you my faith by my deeds. You believe that there is one God. Good! Even the demons believe that—and shudder.

You foolish person, do you want evidence that faith without deeds is useless? Was not our father Abraham considered righteous for what he did when he offered his son Isaac on the altar? You see that his faith and his actions were working together, and his faith was made complete by what he did. And the scripture was fulfilled that says, "Abraham believed God, and it was credited to him as righteousness," and he was called God's friend. You see that a person is considered righteous by what they do and not by faith alone.

In the same way, was not even Rahab the prostitute considered righteous for what she did when she gave lodging to the spies and sent them off in a different direction?

(James 2:14-25 NIV)

"If you love me, keep my commands."

(John 14:15 NIV)

"Your love for one another will prove to the world that you are my disciples."

(John 13:35)

REFLECT

Years ago I heard a pastor say, "Many Christians are educated beyond their level of obedience." It was one of those statements that I had to mull over and over and over. He went on to say, "For some of you, the last thing you need is another Bible study. You need to get busy doing what you already know." That resonated with me deeply. I'd seen it—people who professed to have a deep faith, but the evidence of their life didn't seem to support it. More painfully, I'd seen it in my own life. At times I knew more than I was living out. Yikes!

As you read today's passages, you probably noticed what might appear to be a contradiction. First, we read that faith without works is dead. Then we read that we are saved through faith alone. Which is it? Is it faith or works? How are we saved?

Well, dear friends, it's both. This is not an either/or situation but a cause-and-effect one. Our faith is made known through our works. You can do good works without a strong faith, but as James points out, a strong faith will always expose itself through loving deeds. In other words, you can care for others without loving God, but you can't really love God without caring for others.

How have you observed and experienced that statement to be true?

"If you love me, obey my commands."

(John 14:15)

"Your love for one another will prove to the world that you are my disciples."

(John 13:35)

Therefore, if anyone is in Christ, the new creation has come: The old has gone, the new is here!

2 Corinthians 5:17

I will give you a new heart and put a new spirit in you; I will remove from you your heart of stone and give you a heart of flesh.

Ezekiel 36:26

The New Testament makes it clear that it is through faith in Christ that we are saved. When we accept what Jesus did for us at the cross, we surrender our will to God's. At that moment, we begin a process of becoming a new creation. But, friends, remember it is a process. As we walk with Christ, as we fall more and more deeply in love with Him, our works become an outpouring of the transformation happening within us.

It is not James's intent to argue that works are the way to salvation. His goal is to point out that the result of salvation is obedience.

How do John 14:15 and John 13:35 (in the margin) shed light on James's meaning? What does obedience in response to salvation look like?

As you've read the past two days, the primary commands of God are to love Him and to love others and to share Him with the world. That's the assignment. Deeds are an outer reflection of an inner transformation. As we are shaped into the image of God and grow in that relationship, our lives will bear fruit as evidence.

Read 2 Corinthians 5:17 and Ezekiel 36:26 (in the margin). What do these passages say about transformation?

What specific fruit or traits would you expect to find in the life of a believer who is mature? (For example, understanding of Scripture, sacrificial giving, kind spirit.)

When I was leading a church membership class years ago, a man in the back spoke up and said, "I have to say that I feel a great deal of conviction in this moment." I was surprised because it was not a heavy topic. We were just sharing our gifts and abilities and how we might find joy in ministry. He said, "I can quote large portions of Amos and Obadiah. I even got a theology degree in my spare time out of my interest in the things of God. But the idea of serving someone else has actually never occurred to me."

It was a vulnerable moment from this gentleman. He continued, "Perhaps I have missed the point of what I have studied altogether."

Immediately what came to my mind was the quote I'd heard so many years ago, "Many Christians are educated beyond their level of obedience." This man, in a moment of revelation, realized this was true of his life. The question then became, What would he choose to do?

Someone with that much biblical training would be such an asset. Maybe he could lead studies for adults—perhaps an apologetics study—or help do research for sermons. What would someone with this much education be able to contribute? I was excited about the possibilities, and we talked about many. But to my knowledge, he never has served in the church in any way. It seems he just didn't want to.

I get it. You probably do too. Sometimes we just don't want to do things. People can be difficult. Commitment can be scary. We like to do what we like to do. But when we surrender our will to God's, we give Him permission to put us into action—whenever and however He chooses to do so.

Let's make this personal for you. What has God gifted you to do? What abilities do you have? Those are two different questions, by the way. For instance, you may not be gifted with administration, but you could help address envelopes. Or, you may not be a great cook, but you could deliver meals cooked by others.

List things you do well here (e.g., singing, cooking, working with children, organizing, handling finances, and so forth.):

List abilities you have here (e.g., holding bulletins, holding babies, directing traffic, writing cards, cleaning floors, and so forth):

How might you use a few of the things listed above to bless others and honor God?

We do not earn salvation through good deeds. Our good deeds are an outpouring of our salvation and our love for Jesus. I used to tell my children to imagine themselves a pitcher (not the baseball kind, but the kind that holds water). Our pitchers are full of ourselves (get the pun?). They, meaning we, are full of our selfish wants, needs, and desires. But when we ask Jesus into our hearts, we begin to pour those out and replace them with God's good desires. The goal is to empty our pitchers entirely of selfish ambitions so that we may be filled with God's Spirit and will. And then, as we walk closely with Him, we begin to overflow and splash Jesus everywhere we go. That is a life thriving in Jesus!

As you go out today, may you be so full of Jesus that you splash His goodness everywhere you go. Splish splash!

PRAYER

Lord, forgive me when I do things trying to earn my way into heaven. I know that it is through Jesus alone that I can receive forgiveness of my sins and eternal life. Draw me to You and fill me to overflowing with Your Spirit. I want to splash loving-kindness and acts of generosity everywhere I go. I love You, Lord. Help me love You more! Amen.

DAY 5

SETTLE

Before settling into your time with God today, stand up and stretch. Lift your arms overhead and take in a deep breath. Then exhale slowly.

FOCUS

You foolish person, do you want evidence that faith without deeds is useless? Was not our father Abraham considered righteous for what he did when he offered his son Isaac on the altar? You see that his faith and his actions were working together, and his faith was made complete by what he did. And the scripture was fulfilled that says, "Abraham believed God, and it was credited to him as righteousness," and he was called God's friend. You see that a person is considered righteous by what they do and not by faith alone.

(James 2:20-24 NIV)

"Now go, for I am sending you to Pharaoh. You must lead my people Israel out of Egypt."

But Moses protested to God, "Who am I to appear before Pharaoh? Who am I to lead the people of Israel out of Egypt?" . . .

But Moses again pleaded, "Lord, please! Send anyone else."

(Exodus 3:10-11; 4:13)

The eyes of the Lord search the whole earth in order to strengthen those whose hearts are fully committed to him.

(2 Chronicles 16:9a)

Then I heard the voice of the Lord saying, "Whom shall I send? And who will go for us?"

And I said, "Here am I. Send me!"

(Isaiah 6:8 NIV)

*The word of the L*ORD *came to Jonah son of Amittai: "Go to the great city of Nineveh and preach against it, because its wickedness has come up before me."*

*But Jonah ran away from the L*ORD.

(Jonah 1:1-3a NIV)

REFLECT

We are living in a tough season for the church worldwide. Political division, wars, economic crisis, supply-chain issues, food shortages, and sickness have created an environment where people are volatile. The world is often hurting and angry. And as a result, there is growing skepticism toward anyone or anything in authority, including the church—including God.

That kind of atmosphere is ripe for spiritual rot. Sustained anger and disillusionment can create moral decay and cause a falling away from Jesus. In these times it is especially critical that we double-down on being people of action in the world. We need to tune our ears toward God and report for duty. Here we are Lord, ready for duty!

I live in a military town. Many of my closest friends are, or have been, officers. At the beginning of their military careers, they each voluntarily chose to be commissioned. They signed up and took an oath to protect what they represent and to follow orders immediately. Imagine if, after being commissioned, their superior officer gave them an order and they said, "How about finding someone else to do that?" or "Nah, I don't think I'll do that one." Now, I don't know everything about our armed services, but I'm pretty sure that would not go over well at all!

Or for those of you who are married, what if you were faithful in your marriage most of the time. A spouse who is faithful 90 percent of the time is known as an unfaithful spouse. Commitment is meant to be absolute. Likewise, when you commit to Christ, you are signing on, being commissioned, saying yes in advance to Jesus. "Whatever, whenever, wherever, Jesus, I am available."

James knew that for the church to thrive, believers must be willing to live out their commitment to Jesus. Like us, the environment in which they found themselves was a tough one. We have sickness and political division;

they had persecution and fear of being killed. Yet James encouraged them not to be discouraged but to persevere and put their faith into action anyway!

Reread James 2:20-24 (page 98). Why was Abraham's faith credited to him as righteousness?

Reflect on 2 Chronicles 16:9a. What are your thoughts as you imagine God searching the earth to find people who are faithful?

All followers of Christ are called to be on mission. We are to live out our faith in real and practical ways. God speaks to all His children and sends us on unique missions. But not all who are sent respond willingly.

Throughout Scripture we see three common responses to God's call. These are illustrated well in the lives of Jonah, Moses, and Isaiah. Let's take a look at each one and see what we can learn.

First, there is Jonah, an Old Testament prophet. This is a guy who walked closely with the Lord. So close, in fact, that God instructed him to do something bold in a neighboring town.

Reread Jonah 1:1-3a (page 99). What did God want Jonah to do, and why? What was Jonah's response?

God told Jonah clearly what he wanted Jonah to do, and Jonah's response was essentially, "I'm yours God, but I'm not going."

Initially, Jonah didn't go. He ran the other direction, and as the Book of Jonah tells us, his life was filled with strife because of it. First, the ship he was on was caught in a terrible storm, so the sailors tossed him over to calm the seas (Jonah 1:4-15). Then he was swallowed by a big fish—and eventually vomited up (Jonah 1:17; 2:1-10). It took a lot to get his attention, but eventually he gave in and did what God had called him to do. He went to Nineveh as instructed (Jonah 3:1-3).

When has God spoken to you and you chose not to do what He said (at least at first)?

The second response we often see when God calls someone to serve is demonstrated through Moses. We know him as the great deliverer of the Hebrew people. But Moses didn't start out with a confident response to God's instructions.

Reread Exodus 3:10-11; 4:13 (page 98). What did God ask Moses to do, and what was his response?

> All followers of Christ are called to be on mission. We are to live out our faith in real and practical ways.

God asked Moses to lead His people out of Egypt, and Moses's initial response was basically, "I'm yours God, but send someone else."

Moses didn't refuse to go as Jonah had; instead, he wanted to look for other alternatives. He pled before the Lord, "Please send someone else, anyone else. Not me, Lord!" But like Jonah, he too finally agreed to do what God had asked.

When has God spoken to you and you responded by making excuses?

Then there is Isaiah. He too did not feel worthy in God's eyes, but as he called out to the Lord, his faith was encouraged.

> **Read Isaiah 6:1-7. Why did Isaiah feel unworthy (v. 5)? What happened to give him courage (vv. 6-7)?**

> **Now reread Isaiah 6:8 (page 98). What did God ask, and how did Isaiah respond?**

When God asked whom He could send, Isaiah was ready. His response is the gold standard. He said, "I'm yours, God, send me!"

> **When has God spoken to you and you immediately responded in faith?**

When I was a teenager, I was in a terrible wreck. The passenger side of the car was destroyed, my knees crushed the dashboard, and my head went through the windshield. The car was completely totaled. I, on the other hand, experienced only some cuts and bruises. As I sat alone waiting for the ambulance, I pondered the miracle around me. I had been protected. It was in that moment, and in the days following the wreck, that I made a promise to the Lord. It went something like this:

Lord, thank you for sparing my life. I want to use whatever time I have left serving you. So, in advance I say, "Yes, Jesus. Wherever, whenever, and whatever you want me to do, I say yes. Help me have the courage to follow through with my yeses. Amen.

It was a naive prayer of a thankful sixteen-year-old, but I meant it. And I have tried to keep that vow. But I have to be honest and tell you that I've had my moments like Jonah and Moses too. There have been times when, like Jonah, I just didn't want to do what God was telling me. At other times, like Moses, I just wanted someone else to do the hard thing. Sometimes I have missed it. Sometimes I've gotten it wrong. But I can honestly say I'm trying, and that's what I want you to do—to really try to be the one who says, "I'm yours God, send me!"

What is the last thing God called you to do? What was your response?

Jonah and Moses eventually came around and, like Isaiah, chose to do what God had called to them to do. Sometimes we stumble, but how sweet it must be in the Lord's eyes when we respond like Isaiah, "I'm yours, Lord. Use me. Send me." How beautiful it must be to God when we want our deeds to match our faith.

At the beginning of the week, I challenged you to reach out to your pastor. Did you do it? If not, it's not too late. Make the call and show up. Be someone both God and your church can count on. Let's put our faith into action and fulfill the call that James issued thousands of years ago—a call to be believers who don't just hear the word but also do what it says!

PRAY

Lord, today I am praying a life-altering prayer. I have made my choice. I choose You. However, whenever, wherever, and whatever You want me to do, I say yes in advance, Lord. Help me get rid of my excuses, my fears, and anything that might hold me back from serving You and others with my whole heart. I want my faith to be reflected in how I live, Jesus. Amen.

Action

Living a Life Where Actions Match Faith

Do not merely listen to the word, and so deceive yourselves. Do what it says.
(James 1:22 NIV)

What are three things that you heard about how bees thrive that feel relevant to your Christian life?

1.

2.

3.

Faith that is not accompanied by _____ is dead.

In the good and the bad times of life, we are to be _____. And real faith is backed up with a life filled with _____ _____.

Week 4

CONTROL

Taming the Tongue

Memory Verse

If you claim to be religious but don't control your tongue, you are fooling yourself, and your religion is worthless.

(James 1:26)

DAY 1

SETTLE

Embrace silence today as you focus your full attention on God. Meditate on this verse: "Be still, and know that I am God!" (Psalm 46:10). Simply be still and allow God to meet you in this moment.

FOCUS

Make time this week to read through the entire Book of James once again. (You'll recall that it is only five chapters.)

If you claim to be religious but don't control your tongue, you are fooling yourself, and your religion is worthless.

(James 1:26)

Keep your tongue from evil
and your lips from telling lies.
(Psalm 34:13 NIV)

Set a guard over my mouth, LORD;
keep watch over the door of my lips.
(Psalm 141:3 NIV)

Too much talk leads to sin.
Be sensible and keep your mouth shut.
(Proverbs 10:19)

What you say flows from what is in your heart.
(Luke 6:45b)

REFLECT

As a teenager, one of my heroes made a passing remark that changed my life. He said, "Jennifer, you should consider Christian Education. I think you'd be really good at it."

That's all. That was the whole conversation. My guess is that he doesn't even remember making the comment. But I do. It shaped the trajectory of my life. His words, even though a casual statement, gave me courage to develop a dream. And when I doubted myself, I thought of him. He believed in me and that I could do this.

On the other hand, I also remember those who spoke careless words to me as a child. Things like, "You're not smart enough for that class," "You're not pretty like your cousin," "You're too clumsy to do that," on and on the list goes. Again, I doubt the ones who spoke those words remember doing so, but I do.

Our theme this week is all about controlling our words. This seems so simple, but as I've said before, simple is not always easy. As you dig into God's words this week, you will see that your words reflect your heart and, therefore, are a really big deal. You'll also discover that your words have tremendous power. They can build up, and they can destroy. Simply put, words matter—a lot!

Your words have tremendous power. They can build up, and they can destroy.

Reread each passage (page 107) and record your thoughts about it in the space provided:

Psalm 34:13

Psalm 141:3

We've seen that in the letter we're studying today. James, Jesus's half-brother and the leader of the early church in Jerusalem and beyond, wrote to believers living in a difficult time of persecution when they were literally hunted and killed for their faith—just as Christ followers living in many places in the world today are persecuted. James wrote this letter to encourage them and to instruct them in how to live boldly as Christians so that they could not only survive but also thrive in their situation.

To assist them, James gave practical instructions about how they were to live out their faith. This letter is much more practical than theological. It drops one truth bomb after another, such as the passage we focused on last week: "When troubles of any kind come your way, consider it an opportunity for great joy. For you know that when your faith is tested, your endurance has a chance to grow" (James 1:2-3).

Other moments in the highlight reel of the first chapter of James include:

If any of you lacks wisdom, you should ask God, who gives generously. (1:5 NIV)

Do not merely listen to the word, and so deceive yourselves. Do what it says. (1:22 NIV)

Religion that God our Father accepts as pure and faultless is this: to look after orphans and widows. (1:27 NIV)

These are all memory verse worthy. Although simply stated, they are rich and deep teachings of the faith. And tucked in among these instructional gems in the first chapter of James we find James 1:26:

If you claim to be religious but don't control your tongue, you are fooling yourself, and your religion is worthless.

It's another drop the mic moment. James is saying, if you can't control what you say, your religion is worthless. Boom! In this time of crisis, when danger was real, James clearly stated that words matter.

At first glance this verse seems oddly placed to me. In comparison to matters of faith, action, care of the poor, and persecution, why worry about words? Because words matter!

How have careless words impacted you? Share an example or two below.

How have encouraging words impacted you? Share an example or two below.

Who might you have wounded with careless words? How might you make that right?

Learning how to control my tongue and how to use words in positive ways is a lesson I've been learning my whole life. In fact, one of my life verses is Proverbs 10:19.

Reread Proverbs 10:19 (page 107). What warning and instruction do we find in this verse?

This was one of the first verses I committed to memory. It is so practical, and it resonates deeply with me. As a person who uses a lot of words, I have learned the hard way that careless words can cause a great deal of damage to others—and to my testimony. Whether it's gossip, sarcasm, foul language, a snippy response, or just an unkind word, there really is no place for it in the life of a mature believer. I have found this verse playing through my mind often. When I start to offer a quick comeback, or get in on gossip, or in frustration sound off, I hear these words in my head: "'He who holds his tongue is wise.' Be wise, Jen. Stay quiet!"

Do I get it right all the time? Nope! But I am doing better.

I really hate that words I have spoken in the past have hurt people, and I bet you feel the same way. Perhaps, just like me, you want to do better, much better. Well, we can! It will require intentionality, surrender to the Holy Spirit, and choosing to hold ourselves accountable. But with God's help we can do it! As Luke 6:45b tells us, "What you say flows from what is in your heart." So, if we're going to work on our words, we begin with our hearts. We must come to terms with the fact that our words truly are a reflection of the deepest part of us.

Friends, I hope that you will do the hard, honest work of getting real with yourself about how you use your words. This week has the potential to make your life, your family, your friendships, and your testimony better—immediately. You can do it! Remember, words matter!

PRAY

Pray these Scriptures back to your Heavenly Father today. (I have personalized the first one to match the second one.)

Help me to keep my tongue from evil
and my lips from telling lies.
(Psalm 34:13, author's paraphrase)

Set a guard over my mouth, LORD;
keep watch over the door of my lips.
(Psalm 141:3 NIV)

DAY 2

SETTLE

If time allows, take a walk with the Lord before you do your devotional lesson. Just as you would walk with a friend, chat with Jesus about how you're doing and then listen for what He may want to speak to your heart.

FOCUS

Not many of you should become teachers, my fellow believers, because you know that we who teach will be judged more strictly. We all stumble in many ways. Anyone who is never at fault in what they say is perfect, able to keep their whole body in check.

When we put bits into the mouths of horses to make them obey us, we can turn the whole animal. Or take ships as an example. Although they are so large and are driven by strong winds, they are steered by a very small rudder wherever the pilot wants to go. Likewise, the tongue is a small part of the body, but it makes great boasts. Consider what a great forest is set on fire by a small spark. The tongue also is a fire, a world of evil among the parts of the body. It corrupts the whole body, sets the whole course of one's life on fire, and is itself set on fire by hell.

All kinds of animals, birds, reptiles and sea creatures are being tamed and have been tamed by mankind, but no human being can tame the tongue. It is a restless evil, full of deadly poison.

With the tongue we praise our Lord and Father, and with it we curse human beings, who have been made in God's likeness. Out of the same mouth come praise and cursing. My brothers and sisters, this should not be. Can both fresh water and salt water flow from the same spring? My brothers and sisters, can a fig tree bear olives, or a grapevine bear figs? Neither can a salt spring produce fresh water.

(James 3:1-12 NIV)

Wounds from a friend can be trusted,
but an enemy multiplies kisses.

(Proverbs 27:6 NIV)

REFLECT

Have you ever had someone who loves you speak truth to you and it felt like you had been physically struck? I have, and it stings. It's the kind of sting you can get mad about. You can stew about it, justify yourself, and compare yourself to others in order to rationalize your behavior. Or, you can examine yourself and look for truth. In short, you can allow it to make you bitter or better.

I'm going to be vulnerable with you, friends. In college, one of my roommates sat me down and said, "You know, for someone who is majoring in Christian Education, your language isn't a very good testimony." It felt like she had slapped me in the face. My immediate thought was "Oh, and you think you've got it all together?" I began to think of all the people who had much worse language, who gossiped, who were negative, who were chronic complainers, who were mean spirited. Then, I zeroed in on my roommate. She had stuff wrong in her life too. If she was going to point out my faults, it seemed only fair to return the favor.

But I didn't, because there was truth in what she said. My friend loved me, and her concern was for me and my testimony. Her words were convicting, embarrassing, and painfully true.

> **Reread Proverbs 27:6 above. Who has spoken a hard truth to you?**

> **What was your initial reaction?**

*Every word of God
proves true.
He is a shield to all
who come to
him for protection.
Do not add to his words,
or he may rebuke
you and expose you
as a liar.*

Proverbs 30:5-6

---

*Work hard so you can
present yourself to
God and receive his
approval. Be a good
worker, one who does
not need to be
ashamed and who
correctly explains the
word of truth.*

2 Timothy 2:15

How has it impacted you long-term?

The first twelve verses of James 3 give vivid illustrations of how our words direct our entire lives. The bit in a horse's mouth, rudder of a ship, and small spark have the potential for great power. And, as we saw yesterday in James 1:26, those who are not responsible with their words have a religion that is worthless. Worthless—what a strong word. The translation of this word in Greek includes the meanings "futile," "empty," and "useless." It's a strong verse, and to emphasize his point, James elaborates in chapter 3.

This chapter begins, "Not many of you should become teachers, my fellow believers, because you know that we who teach will be judged more strictly" (James 3:1 NIV). Let's stop right there, because, ouch! For those of you facilitating a group, leading a home study, teaching a Sunday school, or serving in a ministry, this is scary. It reminds me of the Spider-Man mantra: "With great power comes great responsibility." (Any Marvel fans out there?)

For the early church, the gospel was spread through word of mouth. The New Testament had not yet been compiled. Documents to teach people what it looked like to follow Christ were not available, so the spoken word was extremely important. Words were the primary way people came to Christ. It was critical that believers spoke with accuracy and love, for as we read in the Letter to the Romans, "Faith comes from hearing, that is, hearing the Good News from Christ" (10:17).

Read the verses in the margin and paraphrase them in your own words:

Proverbs 30:5-6

2 Timothy 2:15

Speaking truth without embellishment, without inserting personal opinion or adding truths from other sources, is a gift to those around you. And this is especially true when it comes to Scripture because words are still the primary way that people come to a saving relationship with Christ. Our words, even when true, must also be flavored with large amounts of kindness and respect.

Establishing a reputation as someone whose words can be trusted to be both truthful and kind is a key component of spiritual maturity. It paves the way for people to come to us as they seek truth.

Read the following verses and rewrite them in your own words:

Each of you must put off falsehood and speak truthfully to your neighbor. (Ephesians 4:25 NIV)

We will speak the truth in love, growing in every way more and more like Christ. (Ephesians 4:15)

Better is a poor person who walks in his integrity than one who is crooked in speech and is a fool. (Proverbs 19:1 ESV)

As we continue this week in our theme of using our words to help us thrive in life, we will see that our language has the power to build up and to destroy. It can lead people to Christ or be a deterrent from Him. Words

direct our lives, families, careers, marriages, and churches. No wonder James uses such strong language on the topic.

Let your speech be a blessing to those around you, and may your words bring a smile to the face of God.

> **Let your speech be a blessing to those around you, and may your words bring a smile to the face of God.**

PRAY

As you go to God in prayer today, take a few moments to consider your reputation when it comes to how you use your words. Repent for where you've blown it. Request help where you need it. And rejoice in what God has done and will do through your words!

DAY 3

SETTLE

To center your attention fully on God today, pray this Scripture back to Him, personalizing it:

Trust in the LORD with all your heart,
and do not lean on your own understanding.
In all your ways acknowledge him,
and he will make straight your paths.
(Proverbs 3:5-6 ESV)

FOCUS

When we put bits into the mouths of horses to make them obey us, we can turn the whole animal. Or take ships as an example. Although they are so large and are driven by strong winds, they are steered by a very small rudder wherever the pilot wants to go. Likewise, the tongue is a small part of the body, but it makes great boasts. Consider what a great forest is set on fire by a small spark.
(James 3:3-5 NIV)

I tell you, on the day of judgment people will give account for every careless word they speak.
(Matthew 12:36 ESV)

A good man brings good things out of the good stored up in his heart, and an evil man brings evil things out of the evil stored up in his heart. For the mouth speaks what the heart is full of.
(Luke 6:45 NIV)

REFLECT

What part of the body do you think gets people in trouble the most often? It's a weird question, I know. Immediately, your thoughts might go to a sexual part of the body, and that would be a good answer. Or, maybe you're thinking it's the heart, because if our hearts aren't pure, then surely, we'll find ourselves in a lot of trouble. Also, a great answer. But in keeping with our study this week, perhaps the most troublesome part of our bodies is the small muscle we call the tongue.

The entire Book of James reads almost like a pastoral care sermon. His advice and encouragement are both personal and practical. Dealing with problems, using wisdom, practicing humility, caring for others, and spending time in prayer are all part of his instructions for how the church is to behave in order to bring glory to God. But he gets very specific when it comes to the use of the tongue. James knew that despite all our righteous actions, if we cannot control our words, our testimony will be worthless—or perhaps worse than worthless, because when believers don't handle their words well, it actually damages the kingdom of God.

As a person who has served a long time in ministry, I have experienced firsthand more damage to relationships by gossip, mean-spirited language, and backbiting than perhaps any other sin. And when that damage is done by a Christian, it doesn't just affect that individual; it affects the testimony of believers worldwide. After all, we're a family. It gives the family a bad reputation. No wonder James devoted a significant portion of his letter to addressing the tongue.

If we want to grow up into Christ, then we must become masters of our own mouths. Perhaps there is no other mirror that so quickly and accurately reflects our spiritual maturity than does our use of words. Notice that even James, Jesus's half-brother and a leader of the first-century church, did not exclude himself from needing to tame the tongue. He writes, "For we all stumble and sin in many ways. If anyone does not stumble in what he says [never saying the wrong thing], he is a perfect man" (James 1:2 AMP).

Words are powerful. Tomorrow we will see that with our words we can bring both life and death, encouragement and discouragement. But today we will explore how they direct our life and reflect the depth of our faith.

When have you recently stumbled in what you said, saying the wrong thing? Whom did it affect?

Circle the ways in which you are most likely to stumble with words:

Gossip	Lying	Sarcasm
Criticism	Cursing	Yelling
Unkindness	Backbiting	Accusations
Demeaning	Condescending	Mean-spiritedness

Pick one to work on this week:

_____

My husband, Jim, is a horse guy. His days off are usually spent on a trail, riding his precious Egyptian Arabian, Seri. It's amazing to watch them. After years together, she moves in tune with him. The slightest movement of the rein signals her, through the bit in her mouth, which way he wants to go. This thousand-pound animal has been trained to respond quickly to each little nudge. They love and trust each other, and the result is a smooth, gentle experience of being together—most of the time.

Occasionally, something will spook Seri. If a deer or an alligator jumps out at them—yes, both have happened—she runs. And that can be a dangerous situation. It's in those moments of unexpected stress that a tiny appliance in her mouth, known as a bit, becomes especially important. The few times that she panicked, Jim applied great pressure to one side of the bit and that brought her under his control again. Without the bit, she could run out of control, and the result could be disastrous for both of them. The bit gives direction and controls the horse, especially in times of confusion or stress.

I recently asked Jim to give me a few more riding lessons. During my second session, Seri was especially high spirited. It spooked me. In fact, I was ready to quit very quickly. But Jim said, "Use the bit. Pull hard to one side. You've got to maintain control of the mouth."

I've thought of that often. You've got to control the mouth.

In times of stress, how do you tend to react verbally?

Read again Luke 6:45 (page 117). What can you do to intentionally fill your heart with what is good and pure?

What is a practical way you can choose in advance to use your words the next time you are in a difficult situation? (Feel free to borrow my life verse, Proverbs 19:10, here!)

James, as the son of a carpenter (or stonemason, as some experts say),[1] knew rural life. He was not a city boy. Growing up in the Galilee region would have meant a life of agriculture and sailing. So, it is no surprise that his illustrations of the horse's bit and the ship's rudder reflect that lifestyle. These would have been familiar tools to his first-century audience, and how they worked would have been widely understood.

The metaphor illustrates that, like the horse and the ship, large things can be steered by a small part. The tongue, like the bit and the rudder, gives direction. Under the guidance of an expert, the bit guides the horse out of danger and leads it where it needs to go. A skilled fisherman will use the rudder to keep the craft on course and away from storms. Similarly, the tongue must be brought under control. A tongue out of control is perhaps one of the most dangerous and damaging things that can happen in the life of a believer.

To put it simply, friends, you have to give God control of your mouth if you want to thrive. It is a struggle for me. It was a struggle for James. And if you're human, it's a struggle for you too. So, join me in making the decision to do our best to use our words in ways that bring God honor—and when in doubt, to be quiet!

PRAY

God, please forgive me when my words have caused You and others pain. Today, I choose to become intentional with what I say and how I say it. Please help me. I'll need Your help, Your wisdom, and lots of self-control. I commit to use my words in ways that honor You. I love You. Help me love You more. Amen.

DAY 4

SETTLE

Ecclesiastes 5:2 tells us to approach God quietly and ready to listen, as opposed to using many words. Read this passage and let your words be few as you sit before the Lord, preparing your heart to be fully in tune to Him.

Do not be rash with your mouth,
And let not your heart utter anything hastily before God.
For God is in heaven, and you on earth;
Therefore let your words be few.

(Ecclesiastes 5:2 NKJV)

FOCUS

Consider what a great forest is set on fire by a small spark. The tongue also is a fire, a world of evil among the parts of the body. It corrupts the whole body, sets the whole course of one's life on fire, and is itself set on fire by hell.

All kinds of animals, birds, reptiles and sea creatures are being tamed and have been tamed by mankind, but no human being can tame the tongue. It is a restless evil, full of deadly poison.

(James 3:5b-8 NIV)

Set a guard, O Lord, over my mouth;
keep watch over the door of my lips!
(Psalm 141:3 ESV)

The words of a man's mouth are like deep waters [copious and difficult to fathom];
The fountain of [mature, godly] wisdom is like a bubbling stream [sparkling, fresh, pure, and life-giving].

(Proverbs 18:4 AMP)

For the word of God is quick, and powerful, and sharper than any twoedged sword, piercing even to the dividing asunder of soul and spirit, and of the joints and marrow, and is a discerner of the thoughts and intents of the heart.

(Hebrews 4:12 KJV)

REFLECT

When I was a little girl, I remember a classmate spilling an entire lunch tray. The whole tray! It made a huge mess. Milk, mixed with chocolate pudding, peas, and pizza went everywhere. I don't know about your elementary school, but in mine this was an invitation for ridicule. I waited for the meaner kids in our class to start hurling their insults. But before anyone could say anything, our teacher stooped down and began to clean up the mess. Then she said with a sweet smile, "If I was giving out an award for the biggest mess of the day, you'd win. We all make messes. Today it was your turn. Tomorrow, I bet it will be mine." Then, she gave my classmate a hug and they finished the cleanup.

No one said a word about the mess at lunch, and there was no teasing that day on the playground, either. This was new. In fact, I remember thinking that the child who dropped the tray looked almost proud about the whole thing. It was hard for me to put it into words at the time, but what I had witnessed was the power of a kind word. It shut down the bullies and protected a classmate from ridicule. Way to go, teacher!

That was many years ago, but it really stuck with me. Words are powerful. If one of the bullies had gotten in the first word, things would have gone so differently. But not that day! Again, way to go, teacher!

James compares our words to fire, where each word has the potential to set entire forests ablaze. That's great imagery. When I read this particular verse, I think of the fire of gossip. A church lady once told me, "It's not gossip if it's true." Well, church lady, you can split hairs on the definition. But whether true or not, if your speech hurts others, then it's wrong! We can call it gossip, backbiting, slander, or just mean-spirited, but careless words have no place in the life of a believer. As we read in Proverbs, our words are to be like life-giving water:

> We can call it gossip, backbiting, slander, or just mean-spirited, but careless words have no place in the life of a believer. . . . Our words are to be like life-giving water.

The words of a man's mouth are like deep waters [copious and difficult to fathom];
The fountain of [mature, godly] wisdom is like a bubbling stream [sparkling, fresh, pure, and life-giving].

(Proverbs 18:4 AMP)

Reread Hebrews 4:12 (page 123). To what is the word of God compared, and what is its function?

The word *double-edged* refers to the ability to have both good and bad consequences. Certainly, words have that power. With them we can build up and we can tear down. The choice—and it is a choice—is ours.

Who has spoken words to you that brought healing and encouragement?

When have words torn you down and caused you pain?

Our church recently hosted a training for volunteer emergency responders. The entire content of the course was about chainsaw usage. I was surprised by that. A whole day on using a chainsaw! But those who coordinate emergency response teams said that the chainsaw can be a powerful tool, especially in times of natural disasters. But it is also deadly. To use it without care, and without skill, is foolish. It's a danger not only to the one using it, but to everyone near them.

Like the chainsaw, words have tremendous power. They have the potential for great healing and encouragement, but they also can bring destruction and pain. With words, we can create, encourage, build up, and give direction. But our words also can destroy, discourage, tear down, mislead, and corrupt.

Do you remember the old childhood chant, "Sticks and stones may break my bones, but words will never hurt me"? Well, that's a lie. Words can hurt very much. In fact, words can tear apart families, friendships, careers, and even churches. So, becoming responsible for what we speak is an important part of spiritual maturity.

Get honest with yourself: When have your words caused pain for others recently?

To whom do you owe an apology for words spoken carelessly as gossip or unkind remarks?

Read the passages in the margin and rewrite them in your own words:

Proverbs 11:9

Proverbs 18:21

With their words, the godless destroy their friends,
    but knowledge will rescue the righteous.
        Proverbs 11:9

The tongue can bring death or life;
    those who love to talk will reap the consequences.
        Proverbs 18:21

The membership covenant in the church I serve asks people to commit to doing several things as members of the body of Christ. The list includes regular attendance, serving weekly, inviting the lost, praying for the leadership, and refusing to gossip.

If there was only one covenant on the list they were going to keep, the one about refusing to gossip would be at the top of my list. Little else does the damage that an unbridled, irresponsible mouth can. We've established that words matter. They are powerful. Like the chainsaw, words can do tremendous good but, when used poorly, they can destroy everything we hold precious. So, dear friends, let's take Psalm 141:3 (ESV) to heart:

> Set a guard, O Lᴏʀᴅ, over my mouth;
> keep watch over the door of my lips!

PRAY

> Lord Jesus, Your word tells us that "the words of a man's mouth are like deep waters [copious and difficult to fathom]; the fountain of [mature, godly] wisdom is like a bubbling stream [sparkling, fresh, pure, and life-giving]." (Proverbs 18:4 AMP). Help my words be life-giving, filled with wisdom and refreshing like a bubbling spring. Keep me from speaking words that are hurtful, being involved in gossip, and causing harm in any way. Help me today to live in a way that pleases You. Amen.

DAY 5

SETTLE

Stand up and take a deep breath in. Reach your hands over your head as you hold your breath, and then slowly exhale and relax. Now, do it again. Invite the Holy Spirit in with each breath, and as you exhale, release the tensions of the day so that you can be fully present with the Lord today.

FOCUS

Everyone should be quick to listen, slow to speak and slow to become angry.
(James 1:19b NIV)

With the tongue we praise our Lord and Father, and with it we curse human beings, who have been made in God's likeness. Out of the same mouth come praise and cursing. My brothers and sisters, this should not be. Can both fresh water and salt water flow from the same spring? My brothers and sisters, can a fig tree bear olives, or a grapevine bear figs? Neither can a salt spring produce fresh water.
(James 3:9-12 NIV)

Create in me a clean heart, O God,
and renew a steadfast spirit within me.
(Psalm 51:10 NIV)

The tongue can bring death or life;
those who love to talk will reap the consequences.
(Proverbs 18:21)

For the mouth speaks what the heart is full of.
(Matthew 12:34b NIV)

Let no corrupting talk come out of your mouths, but only such as is good for building up, as fits the occasion, that it may give grace to those who hear.
(Ephesians 4:29 ESV)

REFLECT

Have you ever read the classic book *The Five Love Languages* by Gary Chapman? It's an interesting premise that helps us to understand how different people best receive love. After reading through it as a young mom, my family did the work to determine which love language resonated most with each of us. In my household, my husband, son, and daughter all turned out to best experience love through words of affirmation. (I'm more of an acts of service gal, but I digress.) To them, words are very important. They remember what is said, and how it is said. It's part of how they feel loved, chosen, and special. When I realized that the people closest to me shared this word-based love language, I decided I better get really intentional with how I spoke.

In fact, I took 1 Corinthians 13, the love chapter, and rephrased it to help me emphasize how intentional I needed to be with words. Rewritten for this purpose, it might read:

My words should be patient and kind. They should not boast or dishonor others. They won't easily express anger or keep up with every hurt. My words will rejoice in truth and never delight in evil. I will use my words to protect, to share hope, and to encourage.

Once we realized how important words were in our home, Jim and I became very intentional with how we used them. I can't say we never lost our cool or shouted in our home. But I can tell you it was very rare. (As a side note, my coping mechanism when I was exasperated was to whisper. My kids quickly learned that when mom begins to whisper, it's time to pay attention. Ha!)

Having an atmosphere of encouragement and kindness became the norm for us. In fact, my kids might tell you we went a little overboard with it because we would not tolerate sarcasm, yelling, or nastiness. But honestly, in a world where there is so much negativity, we decided our home should be a haven of encouragement and kindness. That atmosphere of choosing your words carefully became a way of life. If someone lost their cool, we'd all look at them like they'd lost their mind. Like, *What are you doing? That's not who we are.* Again, we didn't always get it right. But it was and still is very important in how we do life in our home, because we know that to be careless with our words wounds the very people we love most. It's also a terrible example of what following Christ should be.

By taking James's words to heart, being quick to listen and slow to anger (1:19), we, as women of God, can model a better way of using the gift of words—especially in our homes.

Describe the atmosphere in your home growing up.

What is the atmosphere of your home now?

What about where you work or go to school—what is that atmosphere like?

Reread James 3:9-12 (page 127) and summarize what James is saying in these verses.

James writes, "With the tongue we praise our Lord and Father, and with it we curse human beings.... Brothers and sisters, this should not be" (James 3:9-10 NIV). Ouch! Is there another passage in the entire Bible that so easily steps on our toes? It sure messes up my pedicure!

If we want to honor God, we have to take James's advice to choose our words carefully. We can't sing songs to Jesus in church and then gossip about the people sitting behind us later that same day. We can't say to our friends and neighbors we love God and then lose our tempers when we get home.

Part of maturing spiritually is learning to manage our mouth. And the key to that is developing a pure heart. In fact, Scripture says that our words show who we really are, "For the mouth speaks what the heart is full of" (Matthew 12:34b NIV). From a pure heart there will flow healing, kindness, and encouragement. So, if we want to get serious about how we use our tongue, we have to get serious about the condition of our heart.

What is your heart full of today? Circle all that apply:

Love	Worry	Kindness	Greed
Joy	Grief	Anxiety	Regret
Anger	Compassion	Faith	Jealousy
Bitterness	Sadness	Lust	Peace

Take a look at what you've circled. If you're not pleased with the health of your heart, then pray what David did when he found himself broken before the Lord:

Create in me a clean heart, O God,
and renew a steadfast spirit within me.
(Psalm 51:10 NIV)

Ask God to help you develop a clean heart before Him. You may want to write your prayer here:

In Ephesians 4:29 (ESV), we read, "Let no corrupting talk come out of your mouths, but only such as is good for building up, as fits the occasion, that it may give grace to those who hear."

This is a tall order. Let no corrupting talk come out of your mouth. Let's nail that down specifically. Corrupt talk includes gossip (whether it's true or not), slander, cursing, degrading comments, slurs, sarcasm, lying, mean-spirited talk, backbiting, unconstructive criticism, or expressing opinions for the purpose of stirring people up. None of this has a place in the life of believers! It doesn't matter if it's in person, in writing, or on social media. As James would say, brothers and sisters, this should not be!

Reread Proverbs 18:21 (page 127). What happens to those who love to talk?

I began to wonder what consequences my tongue brought to those I speak to. When my friends see the text bubble come up from my name, do they think it will be an encouraging or discouraging message? I decided it was time to double down on being an encourager.

What about you? Are you ready to double down on being an encourager? What challenges might you face?

Friends, if the tongue has the power of life and death, let's choose life! We have dedicated an entire week to managing our mouths. In a time when it was challenging to be a follower of Christ, when there were many critical issues to be dealt with by the young church, James made sure that his brothers and sisters in Christ knew that words matter. May we choose to use our words in ways that bring life and hope to those we encounter!

PRAY

Make Psalm 51:1-12 (NIV) your own today as you pray it back to the Lord:

Have mercy on me, O God,
*   according to your unfailing love;*
according to your great compassion
*   blot out my transgressions.*
Wash away all my iniquity
*   and cleanse me from my sin.*

For I know my transgressions,
*   and my sin is always before me.*
Against you, you only, have I sinned
*   and done what is evil in your sight;*
so you are right in your verdict
*   and justified when you judge.*
Surely I was sinful at birth,
*   sinful from the time my mother conceived me.*
Yet you desired faithfulness even in the womb;
*   you taught me wisdom in that secret place.*

Cleanse me with hyssop, and I will be clean;
*   wash me, and I will be whiter than snow.*
Let me hear joy and gladness;
*   let the bones you have crushed rejoice.*
Hide your face from my sins
*   and blot out all my iniquity.*

Create in me a pure heart, O God,
*   and renew a steadfast spirit within me.*
Do not cast me from your presence
*   or take your Holy Spirit from me.*
*   Restore to me the joy of your salvation*
*   and grant me a willing spirit, to sustain me.*

Control

Taming the Tongue

If you claim to be religious but don't control your tongue, you are fooling yourself, and your religion is worthless.

(James 1:26)

Three Steps to a More Attractive Mouth

1. _____ what you want to focus on.

2. _____ yourself in God's word.

3. _____ God and others for help.

Week 5

HUMILITY

Developing the Attitude of Christ

Memory Verse

So humble yourselves before God. Resist the devil, and he will flee from you.

(James 4:7)

DAY 1

SETTLE

Stand and take a deep breath in, raising your hands above your head. Hold that breath a few seconds, and then as you exhale, release the troubles on your mind. Do that a few times as you ask God to make you aware of His Spirit that is both with you and within you.

FOCUS

What is causing the quarrels and fights among you? Don't they come from the evil desires at war within you? You want what you don't have, so you scheme and kill to get it. You are jealous of what others have, but you can't get it, so you fight and wage war to take it away from them. Yet you don't have what you want because you don't ask God for it. And even when you ask, you don't get it because your motives are all wrong—you want only what will give you pleasure.

(James 4:1-3)

"Happy are those who are humble;
they will receive what God has promised!"
(Matthew 5:5 GNT)

"The Son of Man did not come to be served, but to serve, and to give his life as a ransom for many."
(Matthew 20:28 NIV)

Clothe yourselves with humility toward one another, because,

"God opposes the proud
but shows favor to the humble."

Humble yourselves, therefore, under God's mighty hand, that he may lift you up in due time.
(1 Peter 5:5b-6 NIV)

REFLECT

This week I had the opportunity to sit down with several people going through difficult times. One is struggling to get along with coworkers, another has ongoing in-law conflict, the third is in a marriage where both she and her husband have drifted into a state of silent cohabitation. Honestly, each of these people is miserable in their current situation. It was obvious that their pain was real, and my heart hurt for each of them. As I listened and tried to offer whatever wisdom God might bring to mind, this thought kept running through my mind: Pride is at the root of all this!

Pride wasn't the presenting issue, of course. My friends began the conversations from their point of view, which makes sense. They focused on what had been done to them and how they had been hurt in the past. But it occurred to me that what was keeping them trapped in an unhealthy place was that they weren't willing to admit any wrongdoing on their part. Instead of humbling themselves to reconcile, pride had won. And when pride wins, we lose.

Every relationship breakdown may not play out this way. But all too often, the reason we have quarrels and fights among us, as James says, is because of pride.

Before we go any further, let's define the terms "pride" and "humility" in the way we are using them this week:

Pride—thinking of ourselves first; a feeling of being better than others, an unwillingness to be corrected or to admit fault

Humility—thinking of others before yourself; it's not thinking less of yourself but thinking of yourself less often

It's important to define these terms for our usage because they can mean different things in different situations. The English language is weird like that. Humility, for instance, can be associated with being afraid or having no courage or lacking self-confidence. Spiritual humility, however, is not like that at all. It is strength contained in kindness. This is the humility Jesus is referring to when he says, "Happy are those who are humble; they will receive what God has promised!" (Matthew 5:5 GNT)

Similarly, pride can vary in its meanings. Sometimes it can mean to feel good about one's accomplishments or to be proud of your children as they grow and flourish. That's a positive use of the word. However, it also can mean thinking of yourself before others, having a self-righteous attitude, or thinking that you are better than, smarter than, or more entitled than others. This pride is a horrible trap.

The problem is, it's hard to see pride in the mirror. It's one of those sins that creeps up on us. Oh, we can see it in the lives of others, but when it comes to ourselves, pride can be sneaky. It disguises itself in rationalization, self-confidence, intellect, even denial. Pride is an ugly look in the life of a believer, and it certainly does not reflect the character of Christ. Jesus himself said, "The Son of Man did not come to be served, but to serve, and to give his life as a ransom for many" (Matthew 20:28 NIV). And we are to be like Him.

Humility, on the other hand, is a beautiful trademark of the Christian life. Saint Augustine wrote that for those who would follow Jesus, the way "is first humility, second humility, and third humility."[1] You know how Realtors say it's all about location? Well, Augustine said it's all about humility!

> **Humility is a beautiful trademark of the Christian life.**

Reread 1 Peter 5:5b-6 (page 135). What did Peter instruct believers to do, and what did he say would be the result?

With whom do you have the most relationship struggles right now (friend, coworker, family member, etc.)? How might pride play into those struggles?

Reread James 4:1-3 (page 135). What insights do you gather about how pride and jealousy play into our relationships?

As we have seen, the people to whom James was writing were living in a difficult spiritual climate. The persecution from both Roman and Jewish authorities made life dangerous for them. They lived out their faith with real consequences. So, it makes sense that James would need to address how to endure hardships, seek wisdom, and put faith into action. Though controlling the tongue, which we addressed last week, and dealing with pride may seem like petty issues in an atmosphere of persecution, they are not. The reality is that even mature believers struggle with pride from time to time.

Read Proverbs 16:18 (NIV) and underline the consequences of pride.

Pride goes before destruction,
> *a haughty spirit before a fall.*

Have you ever experienced the destructive "fall" that follows pride? If so, describe it briefly below.

> The reality is that even mature believers struggle with pride from time to time.

As I read through James 4 in my Bible, I noticed that I once scribbled in the margin, "Why write this?" Apparently, as I studied this book in the past, it struck me as curious that James felt the need to address humility, pride, and jealousy with the early believers who were living in such a challenging time. But then, apparently, I answered my own question, because written beneath my question are the words, "Points to heart condition and surrender of control."

My guess is that James had heard rumblings about arguments and struggles within some of the churches. (Paul certainly had.) So, he addressed it straight on by pointing to the cause of those fights: evil desires within. He wrote, "You want what you don't have . . . your motives are all wrong—you want only what will give you pleasure" (James 4:2a, 3b). How relevant those words are for us today!

Where might you have wrong motives in your life right now?

How might you humble yourself to find peace this week?

This week we will dig into what it means to surrender control and humble ourselves as Christ did. It's a tall order. But the irony is that in humility there is strength—strength of character, of faith, of relationships, and of conviction. In humility we will thrive as God's children!

PRAY

Ask God to help you truly see yourself in the mirror. Invite and allow Him to continue revealing to you any selfish motives, pride, or jealousy in your life. For you to thrive, friend, you need to surrender all of who you are to Him. Let that begin afresh today!

DAY 2

SETTLE

As you get started today, make a list of all the ways God has blessed you. Let it overwhelm you! God's goodness is vast. Delight in Him and the ways He has showered love on you throughout your life.

FOCUS

"God opposes the proud
but gives grace to the humble."

So humble yourselves before God. Resist the devil, and he will flee from you.

(James 4:6-7)

Is there any encouragement from belonging to Christ? Any comfort from his love? Any fellowship together in the Spirit? Are your hearts tender and compassionate? Then make me truly happy by agreeing wholeheartedly with each other, loving one another, and working together with one mind and purpose.

Don't be selfish; don't try to impress others. Be humble, thinking of others as better than yourselves. Don't look out only for your own interests, but take an interest in others, too.

You must have the same attitude that Christ Jesus had.

Though he was God,
he did not think of equality with God
as something to cling to.
Instead, he gave up his divine privileges;
he took the humble position of a slave
and was born as a human being.

> When he appeared in human form,
>> he humbled himself in obedience to God
>> and died a criminal's death on a cross.
>
> Therefore, God elevated him to the place of highest honor
>> and gave him the name above all other names,
> that at the name of Jesus every knee should bow,
>> in heaven and on earth and under the earth,
> and every tongue declare that Jesus Christ is Lord,
>> to the glory of God the Father.
>>> (Philippians 2:1-11)

REFLECT

So, true story. Yesterday, as I was writing on this week's theme of humility, I went to the mailbox and found a neighbor's small packages delivered to our home instead of theirs. I looked up and saw this particular neighbor, whom we don't know very well, standing in his yard. So I waved and said, "Hey, neighbor, we got your mail." To my surprise the response was, "Bring it over and put in on my porch." This wasn't a big deal, but why not walk over and meet me halfway? Why not say, "Thanks. Would you mind putting it on the porch?" or "Here, let me take those from you."

I'm not proud to say this, but I will be vulnerable and share that it really irritated me. I mumbled under my breath as I walked to their house. Then I tossed the packages onto the porch without hearing even a thank-you. My neighbor just stood there and watched me walk over. I was irritated, I tell you. (Not my best moment!)

My husband watched the whole thing, and when I got back to our house he laughed and said, "Yup, that was pretty odd. Good thing you're working on humility this week, right?"

Hmph—I wasn't looking for a character lesson. I wanted Jim to be aggravated, too. Again, I realize this is not a flattering story to tell on myself, but I want to be honest with you. This guy treated me like I worked for him or something. I do not. But as my husband and the Holy Spirit reminded me, I do work for the Lord.

As I thought about why I was aggravated, I realized that what I didn't like was that I was treated with no respect. My pride was injured. There was no thank-you, no effort to meet halfway, just an expectation of what I was to do. Sounds so silly reading this back to myself. I have been a Christ follower for many years. Why was my pride even involved in this interaction? All I did was walk a short way and put down some packages! What a simple thing to do.

I don't think of myself as a person who deals with pride, but apparently I do. I mean, I don't mind humbling myself when I choose to, or when someone is going through a hard time; but when someone else chooses humility for me—well, yesterday's interaction tells me I don't appreciate it in that circumstance.

Humility, as we discussed yesterday, isn't thinking less of yourself; it's thinking of yourself less often. It's putting the needs of others ahead of your own. Even if their needs are delivering packages that you received by mistake. Even if you aren't treated with kindness in the process.

When have you had to humble yourself in order to serve someone?

When have you humbled yourself and not felt appreciated for it?

How did that make you feel?

Our memory verse for the week is James 4:7, "So humble yourselves before God. Resist the devil, and he will flee from you." As I've said, humbling myself when I choose to is not a problem, so humbling myself before the Lord isn't usually difficult for me. But humbling myself when others treat me poorly, well, that's where I struggle.

In what areas of your life and in what settings do you struggle most with humility?

In Philippians 2:3-4 (NIV), Paul encourages believers, "Do nothing out of selfish ambition or vain conceit. Rather, in humility value others above yourselves, not looking to your own interests but each of you to the interests of the others." Valuing others and their interests above ourselves and our interests is challenging enough, but then Paul goes a step further, suggesting what seems a lofty goal.

> Humility isn't thinking less of yourself; it's thinking of yourself less often.

Read Philippians 2:5-8 (NIV) and underline what Paul instructs us to have in our relationships.

In your relationships with one another, have the same mindset as Christ Jesus:

> *Who, being in very nature God,*
> *did not consider equality with God something*
> *to be used to his own advantage;*
> *rather, he made himself nothing*
> *by taking the very nature of a servant, . . .*
> *by becoming obedient to death—*
> *even death on a cross!*

What mindset are we to have? That of Christ! We are to imitate Christ. In the New Living Translation it says, "You must have the same attitude that Christ Jesus had." (Philippians 2:5). Think about that for a moment.

Jesus, God's Son, took on humanity. He gave up the privileges of heaven to become a human and to serve us, to suffer for us, and to give his life in exchange for our own. Surely I can deliver a few packages without an attitude!

How can you imitate Christ in serving others this week?

Since I've already been vulnerable today, let me go all in here. When I work on a mission project, when I travel to Africa and other less developed settings, when I meet people with special needs or someone who is hurting, my humility game is usually strong. In those settings I'm comfortable with humbling myself and serving others. But when I take an honest look at myself—as I'm doing today—I realize that when I serve those who are capable, or are demanding, or have a bad attitude, my humility is lacking. It's much harder to humble yourself before those who either don't appreciate it or seem not to deserve it.

But that is exactly what we are called to do. We are to take on the attitude of Christ, who humbled Himself unto death on a cross for undeserving but very deeply loved people like me and you. Today, take a hard look at yourself in the mirror. In what areas do you need to humble yourself in order to better serve the Lord and others? Remember, God responds to humility with grace (James 4:6)!

PRAY

Lord, forgive me for having prideful attitudes and thinking of my needs before the needs of those around me. Help me to develop Your character of love and humility. Convict me in Your grace and lead and guide me to become the person You created me to be. I love You, Jesus. Amen.

DAY 3

SETTLE

Grab some paper and write down all the things troubling you today. Put it all out there. Now, at least for the duration of today's devotional lesson, just lay those troubles aside. Then, at the end of today's devotional lesson, you'll be invited to turn that list of troubles into a prayer, give the list to God, and then throw it away!

FOCUS

You adulterers! Don't you realize that friendship with the world makes you an enemy of God? I say it again: If you want to be a friend of the world, you make yourself an enemy of God. Do you think the Scriptures have no meaning? They say that God is passionate that the spirit he has placed within us should be faithful to him. And he gives grace generously. As the Scriptures say,

> *"God opposes the proud*
> *but gives grace to the humble."*

So humble yourselves before God. Resist the devil, and he will flee from you.

(James 4:4-7)

REFLECT

My husband and I have a deal. If he's ever around a woman who seems flirty or seems to be getting a little too close (or if I'm around a guy who does the same), we just say to each other privately, "Hey, that makes me uncomfortable." No explanation is needed. The fact that it makes one of us uncomfortable is enough for us to put distance between ourselves and whoever seems to be a threat to our relationship. Our goal is to honor each other and to keep our relationship not only pure but also a safe place where we both feel loved and can thrive. Because of that, anything that could damage our marriage, real or even imagined, is simply off limits. No questions asked. It's not something that happens often; but when it does, protecting our relationship comes first.

God wants the same thing. Anything that could come between you and God should just be off limits. Now don't misunderstand me here. God wants you to enjoy your life, but not at the expense of your relationship with Him, and not by taking advantage of others. This is where humility comes in. We are to humble ourselves by submitting our will to His. In doing that, we receive grace. As we humbly put aside our own wants and desires in order to put God's will first, we receive favor and grace from the Lord. And that grace gives us strength so that we will be able to resist temptations when they come our way.

Read James 4:4-7 again (page 145), and write it below in your own words:

> We cannot love and serve God and love and serve the values of this world at the same time.

We see that James is serious that believers must protect their relationship with God by having no divided loyalties. In James 4:4 he comes out swinging when he writes, "You adulterers! Don't you realize that friendship with the world makes you an enemy of God?"

You adulterers! Ouch! "Adulterer" is not something you want to be called. Unfaithful, disloyal, unchaste—no thanks. Then, he continues to make his point by saying that friendship with the values of this world makes you an enemy of God. Now, you really don't want to be that, an enemy of God—no way!

These are strong images that either get our attention or cause us to quickly dismiss them, thinking they must be written to someone else because they can't possibly be directed at "sweet little old me." Now, we may be sweet, but if we've ever put our wants before God's will, then friends, this verse is for us—for you and for me.

James is clear: We cannot love and serve God and love and serve the values of this world at the same time. One will always overtake the other. And if we're not intentional in keeping God first, the world's values usually win. Part of humility is putting aside our selfish needs and wants (not healthy, God-honoring ones) to place priority on God's desires.

When James writes about friendship with this world, he's not talking about avoiding friendships with people. He means friendship with the values and systems of this world. Wealth, status, power, and convenience are things the world values that God does not want to be a top priority for His children. Now, those things aren't necessarily wrong; there are plenty of people in Scripture who were wealthy, successful, and faithful. The danger is when the pursuit of those things takes precedence over our relationship with Christ. When we allow those desires to become priorities, our loyalties are divided. We become unfaithful, not wholly committed to God. Or as James so pointedly expresses it, we become an adulterer.

James continues in verse 4, "I say it again: If you want to be a friend of the world, you make yourself an enemy of God." Repetition in Scripture signals that something is significant. God is passionate that the Spirit he has placed within us should be faithful to Him.

Faithfulness is a big deal to God! God wants us to be not mostly but wholly committed to Him and to live in ways that honor and reflect that commitment. Again, I think of marriage. When Jim and I got married, our expectation was for 100 percent faithfulness, not 90 or 95 or even 99 percent. You know what you call someone who is faithful 99 percent of the time—unfaithful, a cheater, an adulterer. Because even that 1 percent counts, right? It sure would in my marriage!

So, how do we become wholly committed? Well, humility is the key. The cure for selfish desires is humility. Read that again: The cure for selfish desires is humility. As we humble ourselves to make God's priorities our own, He gives us strength and grace to stand against whatever temptations come our way and to make His agenda our own.

The following Scriptures have both a premise and a promise. The premise is what must be met in order to receive or claim the promise. Dissect each of these passages below:

Humble yourselves before God. Resist the devil, and he will flee from you.

(James 4:7)

Premise:

Promise:

Do not be conformed to this world, but be transformed by the renewal of your mind, that by testing you may discern what is the will of God, what is good and acceptable and perfect.

(Romans 12:2 ESV)

Premise:

Promise:

The reward for humility and fear of the LORD is riches and honor and life.

(Proverbs 22:4 ESV)

Premise:

Promise:

God is faithful. But He expects us to be faithful to Him in return. A spiritual practice that will help you in that pursuit is humility. When times are hard, as they were for the first-century church, we become especially vulnerable to rationalizing our behavior and looking out for our needs above all else. It was in that atmosphere that James warned his brothers and sisters in Christ to resist the devil by taking on the character of Christ through humility. As we put our agenda aside to embrace God's, looking not only to our needs but also to those of others around us, we are practicing humility. The promise here from James is that through humility, evil will be repelled. What a gift!

PRAY

Thank God for His faithfulness and recommit yourself completely to Him. Take on the spirit of humility, seeking God's favor and will above all else. Now, turn the list of troubles you wrote at the beginning of today's lesson into a prayer, throwing the list away. Entrust your troubles to God and go have a fabulous day! (Repeat whenever needed.)

DAY 4

SETTLE

Be still before the Lord and ask Him to search you and lovingly bring to mind anything He may find unhealthy and unpleasing. Get honest before the Lord in preparation for today's focus on drawing near to Him and cleansing ourselves before Him.

FOCUS

Come close to God, and God will come close to you. Wash your hands, you sinners; purify your hearts, for your loyalty is divided between God and the world. Let there be tears for what you have done. Let there be sorrow and deep grief. Let there be sadness instead of laughter, and gloom instead of joy. Humble yourselves before the Lord, and he will lift you up in honor.

(James 4:8-10)

Search me, God, and know my heart;
test me and know my anxious thoughts.
See if there is any offensive way in me,
and lead me in the way everlasting.
(Psalm 139:23-24 NIV)

REFLECT

Every week in our worship service, we give our congregation action steps at the end of the message. We call them the next steps. The goal is that after hearing the sermon and reading the Scriptures, they will move into action by doing something to put the lesson into practice. These actions vary from memorizing a verse, to doing anonymous acts of kindness, to serving in a ministry, and so forth. Some of the next steps are easy; others are tough.

Perhaps the toughest next step we ever issued was from a sermon on getting along with others and the need to humble yourself in order to see situations from their perspective. Here's what we challenged our congregation to do: ask three people with whom you are close, *What is it like on the other side of me?*

What a question! As we quickly found out, our people found it daunting. But they weren't the only ones. I, too, was scared to face the brutal truth.

I didn't want to ask our people to do something that I hadn't already done. So before preaching this particular message, I did the next step in advance. It was terrifying! Separately, I sat down with my husband, a friend, and a coworker and asked the power-packed question, *What is it like on the other side of me?*

For forty-eight hours before sitting down with them, I agonized over what their responses would be. What would they reveal? Could I handle it? Although I knew these people loved me, I wasn't sure I wanted the absolute truth about myself. So, I prayed for courage and humility to hear what I needed to hear and then do something positive with that information.

To my surprise, these conversations were precious. Each of my friends began with things they loved about me. They shared how they saw God's fingerprints in my life, and then, delicately, they shared what they saw as an area of my life that could use some work. It was one of the most humbling experiences of my life. But I believe it made me a better person, a better wife, and a better friend.

As I approached those conversations, these verses we read today came to mind:

> *Search me, God, and know my heart;*
> *test me and know my anxious thoughts.*
> *See if there is any offensive way in me,*
> *and lead me in the way everlasting.*
> *(Psalm 139:23-24 NIV)*

I felt closer to my loved ones and to the Lord as a result of doing the hard work of really looking at myself. By humbling myself and being willing to repent where there was sin, I felt like a cleaner, fresher version of me.

Taking a hard look in the mirror requires both humility and courage. It takes humility to realize that we don't have it all together. We all have areas that need work. And it takes courage to be willing to look at the whole truth and say, "Search me and tell me about myself." And then, when we find out hard truths, it takes humility to do the work of admitting where we need to repent in order to become the most Christlike version of ourselves. But, at the end of the process—if we do the work of humbling ourselves, confronting areas of sin, and then repenting of that sin—we receive the gift promised here: God will lift us up in honor.

Reread James 4:8-10 (page 150). Like the verses we looked at yesterday, these verses contain premises and promises. There are several premises that must be met in order to receive two promises. I've listed the premises for you. Add the promises.

Premises: **Promises:**

Come close to God.

**Purify your hands
and heart.**

**Mourn for what you
have done.**

**Humble yourselves
before the Lord.**

What keeps you from drawing close to God on a regular basis?

When have you felt, or when do you feel, particularly close to the Lord? What was or is special about that time?

What safeguards can you put in place to be focused on staying close to Jesus?

The premises in James 4 are tall orders, but in return there are two amazing promises: God will come close and lift you up in honor! The English Standard Version uses this language: "Draw near to God, and he will draw near to you" (James 4:8a). Drawing near seems to be a clear instruction. But, it's easy for us to fall into spiritual drift. The best way to avoid this is to put spiritual practices in place so that we intentionally focus on our relationship with Christ daily.

What does your spiritual routine look like? What are your spiritual habits?

How effective have these habits been recently in bringing growth? What needs attention?

Then the LORD said to Moses, "Make a bronze washbasin with a bronze stand. Place it between the Tabernacle and the altar, and fill it with water. Aaron and his sons will wash their hands and feet there. They must wash with water whenever they go into the Tabernacle to appear before the LORD and when they approach the altar to burn up their special gifts to the LORD— or they will die!

Exodus 30:17-20

The next part of verse 8 says, "Cleanse your hands, you sinners, and purify your hearts, you double-minded" (ESV). The practice of washing hands in Jesus's day was not only a sanitary ritual but also a ritual of spiritual significance dating back to the time of the Exodus.

Read the verses in the margin. What were the priests to do, and when? What would happen if they did not do this?

In what parts of your life do you struggle to live according to God's will and desires?

Are you ready to be cleansed of that today? If so, pray and ask God to cleanse you now. You may even want to write out your prayer to the Lord.

If you're really feeling gutsy, find a few trusted friends and try out that "next step" by asking them, What's it like on the other side of me?

James suggests that there should be tears for what we have done or not done. He says let there be sorrow and deep grief. Let there be sadness instead of laughter, and gloom instead of joy. His instruction is to actually mourn over our sins. I've done that before. I have been brokenhearted over my sin and bad attitude at times. But let me be honest, sometimes I haven't. Perhaps I have not even been fully aware of my sin. The step that James gives us here is to pause, to mourn, and to repent from anything that would create distance between us and our heavenly Father.

To mourn and repent is an act of humility that paves the path for the ultimate reward: "Humble yourselves before the Lord, and he will lift you up in honor" (James 4:10). I don't fully know what it means for God to lift us up in honor, but I like it. A lot!

Friends, may this be our goal—to draw close, to repent, to mourn our sins, and humble our attitudes in order to be close to God and be lifted up in places of honor with Him! Now, that is thriving!

PRAY

Read this psalm to the Lord today as a prayer for your life:

Search me, God, and know my heart;
Test me and know my anxious thoughts.
See if there is any offensive way in me,
and lead me in the way everlasting.
(Psalm 139:23-24 NIV)

DAY 5

SETTLE

As you quiet your heart, ask God to give you His peace today. You may want to sing a familiar hymn or listen to a favorite song to help usher you into His presence. Allow your focus to be fully on Him.

FOCUS

My brothers and sisters, believers in our glorious Lord Jesus Christ must not show favoritism. Suppose a man comes into your meeting wearing a gold ring and fine clothes, and a poor man in filthy old clothes also comes in. If you show special attention to the man wearing fine clothes and say, "Here's a good seat for you," but say to the poor man, "You stand there" or "Sit on the floor by my feet," have you not discriminated among yourselves and become judges with evil thoughts?

Listen, my dear brothers and sisters: Has not God chosen those who are poor in the eyes of the world to be rich in faith and to inherit the kingdom he promised those who love him? But you have dishonored the poor. Is it not the rich who are exploiting you? Are they not the ones who are dragging you into court? Are they not the ones who are blaspheming the noble name of him to whom you belong?

If you really keep the royal law found in Scripture, "Love your neighbor as yourself," you are doing right. But if you show favoritism, you sin and are convicted by the law as lawbreakers. For whoever keeps the whole law and yet stumbles at just one point is guilty of breaking all of it. For he who said, "You shall not commit adultery," also said, "You shall not murder." If you do not commit adultery but do commit murder, you have become a lawbreaker.

Speak and act as those who are going to be judged by the law that gives freedom, because judgment without mercy will be shown to anyone who has not been merciful. Mercy triumphs over judgment.

(James 2:1-13 NIV)

For God does not show favoritism.

(Romans 2:11)

Do nothing out of selfish ambition or vain conceit. Rather, in humility value others above yourselves.

(Philippians 2:3 NIV)

REFLECT

When our children were younger, Jim and I had the opportunity to speak at a church gathering alongside President Jimmy Carter. It was such an honor to be on the agenda with a former president that we decided to get Alyssa and Josh out of school so that they could meet him, or at least see him from a distance. As presidential occasions go, this one was pretty casual. In fact, at the end of what had been a long day, there was a meal served buffet style by the ladies of the church.

As you'd expect, President and Mrs. Carter were escorted to the front of the line, flanked by their Secret Service officers and other dignitaries in attendance.

We, on the other hand, were in the back of the room, waiting our turn in line. It was then that I noticed our seven-year-old, Josh, was missing. We began to scan the room and to my horror, I saw him cut to the front of the line. Josh was asking President Carter to spoon mashed potatoes on his little wobbly plate! I froze. What's the protocol here? What will the Secret Service do if I run up to the front of the room? It was a casual atmosphere, but rushing a president can't be a good thing in any circumstance. So, I watched as Jimmy and Rosalynn Carter fixed a plate of food for my son, carried it to the table, and helped him get seated.

Once things seemed settled, Jim and I calmly walked up and thanked them. Josh turned to us and said, "I was hungry, so this poppi and mimi helped get my food." Then he said, "And look, their friends have guns! That's so cool."

We were mortified but also really tickled. Our little boy wasn't impressed by who they were and the status they held. What he saw were two grandparent types he figured would help him fix a plate of chicken and potatoes. And they did.

When has someone humbled themselves to serve you? How did it make you feel?

How, and from whom, have you observed humility as strength?

This week our emphasis has been on humility. Although the primary text on humility is found in chapter 4, James has woven the practice of humility throughout the entire letter. Today we will expand our discussion of humility to include the issue of favoritism, which at its core is also about humility.

Reread James 2:1 (page 156). Who is not to show favoritism? How would you define favoritism?

We're all familiar with favoritism and prejudice. Simply put, they are the unfair practices of treating some people with more honor (favoritism) or dishonor (prejudice) than others. My guess is that you have felt the sting of favoritism or prejudice at some point in your own life—maybe many times. In either case, someone or some group is elevated while another is overlooked or mistreated. Whether it stemmed from your race, gender, economic status, or general appearance, if you have been judged harshly, you probably carry some wounds from those encounters. I do.

As we look over the course of human history, we see that favoritism has been more than a little unpleasant. Prejudice has been the cause of hate, wars, and suffering for millions. And that is why God is so clear about His hatred of it.

Reread James 2:9. What does this verse say about those who show favoritism?

James says that if you show favoritism, you sin. Let's hear that again: Favoritism is sin. It is not just a preference or a prejudice from your upbringing; it is sin. And we must face it head-on in order to eliminate it from our lives.

As James instructs the early church in how to live out their newfound faith, he focuses on the importance of a humble spirit that shows no partiality. If we are to be imitators of God and reflect the character of Christ, then this is a requirement.

Reread Romans 2:11 (page 157). Who does not show favoritism?

Unlike us, God does not show favoritism. His grace is available to all people. His love extends to everyone without regard to their station in life, race, sex, wealth, or position of power. Friends, as God's children, we are called to do the same!

Remember John 3:16 (NIV): "For God so loved the world that he gave his one and only Son." It doesn't say, "For God so loved the white people" or "the men." It's not just one race or the rich or the smart or the pretty but the whole world that Jesus came to give His life for.

Look up these passages and record your thoughts as they relate to favoritism in God's eyes:

Acts 10:34-35

Romans 10:9-13

Matthew 10:40

How have favoritism and prejudice affected you personally?

No matter what your political views may be, having a meal with a former president of the United States is pretty cool. President Carter was the leader of the most powerful nation in the world. He lived in the White House and brokered a peace deal between Israel and Egypt. He has dined with the brightest and wealthiest people on the planet. Yet, he also is the guy who helped my son fix his plate at a church dinner.

When Josh approached the president, he never looked around for security. He didn't shoo Josh away or order someone else to help him. And thank goodness, he didn't turn around and say, "Where is this child's mother?" Instead, he let my little boy squeeze in front of him and then helped him with no questions asked. In that moment, he was just a kind man helping a little boy.

Before we left that day, Josh begged us to take a picture of him with his new friends—no, not President and Mrs. Carter, but the Secret Service agents! In his little world, that was who was cool. But for me, Jimmy and Rosalynn Carter were the ones who left a lasting impression. They did not regard their high station in life but gently served a child—a great example of humility in action.

Philippians 2:3 tells us that we should do nothing out of selfish ambition or vain conceit, but in humility we are to value others above ourselves. Friends, when we put the needs of others before our own, when we humble ourselves in order to serve—perhaps it is in those moments that we are most like Jesus.

PRAY

Dear God, show me where I have prejudice and in what ways I am guilty of favoritism. Give me a pure heart to see and love people as you do. Please forgive me when I have been prideful and have hurt others through the sin of favoritism. Make me more like Jesus. I love You, Lord. Amen.

When we put the needs of others before our own, when we humble ourselves in order to serve—perhaps it is in those moments that we are most like Jesus.

Humility

Developing the Attitude of Christ

So humble yourselves before God. Resist the devil, and he will flee from you.
(James 4:7)

"Humility is not thinking _____ of yourself, _____ thinking of yourself
_____."

–Rick Warren

We need to _____ our motives.

_____ ourselves before God.

_____ the Devil.

Week 6

PRAYER

Exercising the Power Tool of the Faith

Memory Verse

The earnest prayer of a righteous person has great power and produces wonderful results.

(James 5:16b)

DAY 1

SETTLE

This week is all about prayer. So, as you settle in for time dedicated to the Lord, try praying in a new posture. You may want to get on your knees, go outside, take a walk with the Lord, or even lay flat before Him. Give Him your undivided attention and simply talk and listen to your heavenly Father.

FOCUS

Is anyone among you in trouble? Let them pray. Is anyone happy? Let them sing songs of praise.

(James 5:13 NIV)

When Jesus had cried out again in a loud voice, he gave up his spirit.

At that moment the curtain of the temple was torn in two from top to bottom. The earth shook, the rocks split.

(Matthew 27:50-51 NIV)

REFLECT

While traveling recently, Jim and I visited a huge food market in Ecuador. The fruits and vegetables were fresh and beautiful. The people were incredibly kind and very patient with our broken Spanish. Thankfully, we had a guide with us who helped us navigate this excursion.

As we gathered our produce and were exiting the market, we noticed a shrine. It was an elaborate setup. There was a beautiful framed picture of Mary surrounded by flowers. Seated beneath the picture was a doll representing Jesus as a toddler. But the scene was odd to us. Jesus was dressed as a little girl in a beautiful golden dress. When we inquired about what was happening, our guide told us that the tradition in the area is to dress baby Jesus in the clothes of the one for whom you are praying. In fact, across the street from the market was a costume store where baby Jesus outfits could be purchased in various forms such as children, doctors, teachers, and farmers. The idea is to dress the doll in a way that God can understand who the prayer is meant to bless.

The whole situation was so strange to us. Now, don't misunderstand me, we didn't have a harsh attitude. We weren't being judgmental. In fact, our hearts were touched by the sincerity and lengths that these precious people felt they needed to go to in order to get God's attention.

I also wondered, What would seem odd to them about how we pray and worship?

As we left the market, I was struck by the idea that all too often we—human beings throughout history—have made trying to get God's attention too complicated. God simply wants us to focus on Him. No rituals are necessary, just an honest heart that is open to communicate with Him.

The One who knows you best, loves you most. He is available. No matter the need, great or small, God is present and ready to listen and respond.

What was prayer like in your home when you were growing up?

What prayer practices have you experienced that are helpful?

What questions do you have about prayer?

During my teen years, both of my parents worked. My mom was a teacher, so if I needed one of them, I knew it would be hard for her to leave her classroom. My dad, on the other hand, worked in a corporate office and had an administrative assistant. I tried not to interrupt him at work, but sometimes a girl just needs her mama or daddy. There wasn't a phone line that went directly to his office (no cell phones back then), so I would call his assistant, Lisa. As soon as she heard my voice, she would say something like, "Hey, what do you need, honey? I can get him right now."

I loved that no matter how busy he might be, he would stop what he was doing and listen to me. It made me feel loved. It helped me understand what a priority I was, and still am, in his life.

God is the same way. Sometimes we make it complicated. Sometimes we create rituals and rules. Sometimes we design systems such as dressing up dolls as our loved ones. But it just isn't necessary. The One who knows you best, loves you most. He is available. No matter the need, great or small, God is present and ready to listen and respond.

I hope this is not news to you. But for some it may be. God may seem too big, too busy, and too important to be bothered with our concerns. But that is wrong! Like a great parent, God wants to hear from us. He also wants us to listen to Him. This is prayer, both talking and listening to God.

How would you describe your prayer life right now?

How would you like it to be?

You may know that in the Old Testament, direct access to God was limited. God's Spirit was given to certain individuals for specific purposes. And God dwelled in the Holy of Holies within the Temple.

Read 2 Chronicles 3:8-14 and describe in your own words what the Holy of Holies, or Most Holy Place, was like.

This most sacred place within the Temple was a small, square, and windowless enclosure covered in gold and separated from the rest of the Temple by a heavy curtain, or veil. The veil was made of beautiful blue, purple, and scarlet linen and embroidered with golden cherubim. And two golden cherubim stood within the space with their wings touching. (See Exodus 26:33-34.)

Then Jesus shouted out again, and he released his spirit. At that moment the curtain in the sanctuary of the Temple was torn in two, from top to bottom. The earth shook, rocks split apart, and tombs opened.
Matthew 27:50-52a

Once a year at Yom Kippur, also known as the Day of Atonement, the high priest would enter the Holy of Holies to make a sacrifice on behalf of the entire nation of Israel. It was through this process that the nation was cleansed from their sins.

Note that the high priest was the only one with access to the presence of God, but this was before Jesus came to earth.

Read Matthew 27:50-52a (in the margin). What happened when Jesus died on the cross?

When Jesus gave up His spirit, there was an earthquake and the curtain of the Temple was torn from top to bottom. Everything changed in that moment! The curtain, the barrier that protected us from God's presence but also kept us distant, was gone. The cross disposes of the need for animal sacrifice because the perfect sacrifice has been made in Jesus. Ultimate atonement is available through the cross. We no longer need a high priest to intercede on our behalf; we can go to God ourselves! We have direct access to call on the God of the universe at any time!

So, what do we do with that gift? When should we pray and what should we pray about? Everything and anything!

> **Reread James 5:13 (page 165). When and what does James say we are to pray?**

The early believers to whom James addressed this letter were going through many hardships, yet he says they should pray to God at all times, regardless of their circumstances—asking God for help during the hard times and singing praise to Him in the good times.

Tomorrow we'll look more at how to live this out. But for today, just thank God that in the good times and the bad times, He is there for you. He's ready to take the call and wants you not only to tell Him what's on your heart but also to listen to what is on His. You don't have to set up a shrine to get God's attention! The curtain has been torn, the Spirit has been given. God sees you right where you are today and hears your prayer.

Let's make this a week of prayer, friends. And through that prayer, we will thrive!

PRAY

Thank You, God, for the gift of Jesus. Through Him I have access to You directly, and I'm so grateful for that! Help me to understand and appreciate fully what that means. Help me develop my prayer life into one of power and humility. I want to learn to speak and listen in ways that honor You. I love You, Lord. Amen.

DAY 2

SETTLE

Quiet your heart and mind by just being still for a minute, maybe even two. Allow all distractions to fall away and focus entirely on Jesus. Ask Him to reveal Himself to you in new ways as you seek Him today.

FOCUS

The following passage from James is often known as the Prayer of Faith. We will be looking at this Scripture for the next few days.

Is anyone among you in trouble? Let them pray. Is anyone happy? Let them sing songs of praise. Is anyone among you sick? Let them call the elders of the church to pray over them and anoint them with oil in the name of the Lord. And the prayer offered in faith will make the sick person well; the Lord will raise them up. If they have sinned, they will be forgiven. Therefore, confess your sins to each other and pray for each other so that you may be healed. The prayer of a righteous person is powerful and effective.

Elijah was a human being, even as we are. He prayed earnestly that it would not rain, and it did not rain on the land for three and a half years. Again he prayed, and the heavens gave rain, and the earth produced its crops.

(James 5:13-18 NIV)

Pray without ceasing.
(1 Thessalonians 5:17 ESV)

Do not be anxious about anything, but in everything by prayer and supplication with thanksgiving let your requests be made known to God. And the peace of God, which surpasses all understanding, will guard your hearts and your minds in Christ Jesus.

(Philippians 4:6-7 ESV)

"It is the Lord who goes before you. He will be with you; he will not leave you or forsake you. Do not fear or be dismayed."

(Deuteronomy 31:8 ESV)

REFLECT

As a young believer, I struggled with prayer.

I often prayed for things that didn't happen. For instance, one of my friends was in a horrible accident and lost the use of his legs. We prayed. Many, many people prayed. Well-meaning people quoted the verse from James 5 that says if a prayer is offered in faith, then the sick will be healed. We prayed and we believed. But it didn't work. He has never regained the use of his legs.

So, I wondered, Did we do something wrong? Are we not praying correctly? Is there more to this Scripture than what I understand? What are we missing, Lord? But mostly, I wondered, Are You there? And if You are, do You care? I worked through this struggle to learn that God does not say yes to every prayer. (We'll talk more about that in a moment.)

But I had another roadblock. I read Paul's instruction in 1 Thessalonians to pray without ceasing, and it discouraged me. Actually, I think I was more embarrassed than discouraged, because I didn't do that. Honestly, I didn't even know what praying without ceasing meant. I thought, How do you do anything without ceasing except breathe and pump blood? I felt that way for years. Then one day in my twenties I remember thinking that the whole day had been an ongoing conversation with the Lord. I had talked, aloud and silently, and I had listened. Playing with the kids, shopping in the grocery store, doing whatever I did wherever I went, prayer had been a part of my day; and this Scripture came alive. Pray without ceasing—okay, Lord, I can do that!

What is your experience with praying without ceasing? Circle one:

I've never tried it

I do it sometimes, often when I'm struggling

I talk to God all the time

What struggles have you had in your prayer journey?

How have those struggles impacted your faith?

What victories have you experienced through prayer?

How have those victories impacted your faith?

If you have ever had an experience when God appeared to say no or not yet to one of your prayers, then you are in great company. King David, the one God commends for being a man after His own heart, asked God for the privilege to build the Temple. God said no (see 1 Chronicles 28). Or look at Paul, the author of the majority of the New Testament. He pleaded with God three times to take away what he referred to as a thorn in his flesh, but God said no (see 2 Corinthians 12).

Even Jesus had to submit His will to His Father's.

"Father, if you are willing, please take this cup of suffering away from me. Yet I want your will to be done, not mine."

Luke 22:42

Read Luke 22:42 (in the margin). What did Jesus pray as He faced death on the cross?

In this passage we see the attitude we are to have: Pray for whatever is on your heart and mind but be willing to submit to God's will above your own.

We have to understand this as we pray the way James instructs. Not every prayer, even those prayed in faith, is answered exactly as we hope it will be.

Sometimes God says yes and we see what we prayed for happen right away. That's awesome when it lines up that way.

But when we pray and don't receive what we asked when or how we hoped for it, it's easy to believe that God has forgotten us or is too busy to deal with our needs. However, Scripture tells us clearly that God hears us.

Reread Philippians 4:6 and Deuteronomy 31:8 (pageS 170–171). How do these verses encourage you?

In the short term I like it when God says yes to my prayers. But as I look back on my life, I am thankful that all my prayers did not receive an affirmative response. My life would have taken a much different course if every prayer had been answered in the way I asked. For instance, I would have married my high school crush instead of the love of my life. Instead of law school, once a hope and prayer of mine, God led me to vocational ministry. As a result, I've had the opportunity to be involved with thousands of people who have chosen to receive and follow Jesus. God knew best and I'm glad that, at least in those situations, I accepted His will instead of forcing my own. My life is better because of it.

If you have struggled with prayer in the past, and most of us have, then make it your aim this week to run to God with everything on your heart and mind. And no matter how He appears to answer you, trust Him!

> **Even when we don't understand, God is there. And He is always good.**

Even when we don't understand, God is there. And He is always good. His nature is loving, kind, just, and wise. In that wisdom we will sometimes hear a no, or a not yet. But friends, keep seeking Him. Keep praying and remember that the One who knows you best and loves you most wants the very best for you.

PRAY

As you pray today, pour out your heart before the Lord. There may be things you have been praying for over a long period of time: salvation of a loved one, healing, financial breakthrough, or guidance. Lay those before the Lord again today and then just be still. In the same fashion that Jesus prayed, make your request known to God; then end with "yet not my will, but yours be done" (Luke 22:42b NIV).

DAY 3

SETTLE

Get creative today! Draw, sing, write, take a short walk—whatever you choose, do it with God. Spend this creative energy focused on God's goodness, and let your activity be a form of worshipping Him.

FOCUS

Are any of you suffering hardships? You should pray. Are any of you happy? You should sing praises. Are any of you sick? You should call for the elders of the church to come and pray over you, anointing you with oil in the name of the Lord. Such a prayer offered in faith will heal the sick, and the Lord will make you well. And if you have committed any sins, you will be forgiven.

Confess your sins to each other and pray for each other so that you may be healed. The earnest prayer of a righteous person has great power and produces wonderful results.

(James 5:13-16)

Come, let us bow down in worship,
let us kneel before the Lord our Maker.
(Psalm 95:6 NIV)

Finally, be strong in the Lord and in his mighty power. Put on the full armor of God, so that you can take your stand against the devil's schemes. For our struggle is not against flesh and blood, but against the rulers, against the authorities, against the powers of this dark world and against the spiritual forces of evil in the heavenly realms. Therefore, put on the full armor of God, so that when the day of evil comes, you may be able to stand your ground, and after you have done everything, to stand,...

And pray in the Spirit on all occasions with all kinds of prayers and requests. With this in mind, be alert and always keep on praying for all the Lord's people.
(Ephesians 6:10-13, 18 NIV)

REFLECT

When I come home, whether after a long day at work, or a ten-minute trip to the store, there is one thing I can count on—my dog, Sam. He is always ready to enthusiastically welcome me home. Tail wagging, jumping up and down, Sam will be there. He is faithful. No matter what kind of day I've had, he is there ready to love on me and snuggle. If I'm in a bad mood, he doesn't care. He is a constant companion. A faithful friend no matter what's happening.

When he greeted me recently, I had to wonder how long he had been staring at the door just waiting for me to come home. His big eyes looked so happy as I opened the door. As I rubbed his little ears and loved on him, I wondered, Does God wait for us in a similar way?

No matter what we are going through, no matter what our mood, God is ready for us to turn to Him and spend time with Him. Sam is a good reminder to me of that every day.

How does it comfort you to know that God is eager to meet with you at any moment?

James ends his letter to the early church with a plea to face all things through prayer. Is anyone in trouble? Pray. Anyone happy? Pray. Are you sick? Pray. Anyone dealing with sin? Pray. Whatever the situation, James is clear: Prayer is an appropriate response. And in the same way that Sam waits for me, God waits for each of us—enthusiastically waiting for us to turn our attention to Him and simply be with Him!

Let's jump to Ephesians for a moment. It's interesting that when Paul gets to the end of his letter to Ephesus, he, like James, concludes with instructions on prayer.

Reread Ephesians 6:10-13 (page 175). What is the spiritual armor Paul describes? List it below.

Paul describes in detail the armor every believer must be equipped with to fight spiritual battles. He urges us to put on the helmet of salvation, breastplate of righteousness, shield of faith, belt of truth, sword of the Spirit, and shoes of peace. These are to be worn by every believer so that we can stand against the forces of darkness that wage war in this world. This is a well-known passage.

Immediately following these verses on the armor of God is a slightly lesser-known verse.

Now reread Ephesians 6:18 (page 175). What instruction does Paul give here?

> No matter the situation, prayer is the answer.

Paul urges us to pray at all times about all things. Much like James, he concludes his letter with the urgency, the directive, the necessity to make prayer the base upon which we build our lives and face our difficulties. As we have discussed throughout our study, the climate that the first-century believers were living in was tough. Their hardships were numerous. So, James is clear in his directive that whether they were happy, in trouble, sick, or suffering, they were to run to their knees in prayer.

No matter the situation, prayer is the answer.

Think back on a time or season when prayer was especially powerful for you. Where were you? What were you doing? Who was present?

Are there elements of that time that you can reproduce to experience meaningful times of prayer on a regular basis?

As a teenager, my favorite church services were on Sunday evenings. It wasn't the music or the message that I loved, although I'm sure they were good. It was the opportunity to spend time on my knees at the altar that I cherished. Almost every service ended on our knees, and I looked forward to it. During the week I would think about what I would bring to God at the altar. And when the invitation was given, I was ready. It was there that I did serious teenage business with the Lord. Now, I realized I could pray anytime, anywhere, but there was something special about kneeling before the Lord and coming to Him in that humble position.

The practice of praying while in a kneeling position is mentioned frequently in Scripture.

Look up and record your thoughts on these passages that reference the practice of kneeling in prayer:

Psalm 95:6

Daniel 6:10

Luke 5:8

Luke 22:41

Romans 14:11

Psalm 95:6 invites us to worship before the Lord on our knees. In Daniel 6:10, we see that Daniel knelt before the Lord three times a day. Luke 5:8 gives us a picture of humble repentance. Luke 22:41 shows us Jesus's posture in prayer. In Romans 14:11, Paul reminds us that one day every knee will bow and every tongue confess that Jesus is Lord.

Kneeling before God is an act of reverence and humility. It also has been my experience that while on my knees, my mind is not likely to wander. Kneeling, at least for me, is not a particularly pleasant position. It's a little—sometimes a lot—uncomfortable, and that helps keep my mind focused on why I'm down there. Kneeling conveys, in a tangible way, that this moment is different. This moment is set aside to communicate with God.

If you're physically unable to kneel, then consider what position of humility you could assume before the Lord. There are other postures and ways to take on a position of humility before the Lord. The goal is not the kneeling but the dedicated time focused on God.

If you are physically able to kneel, how does this posture help you to humble yourself before the Lord?

If you are physically unable to kneel, what are some other postures and ways you can take a position of humility before the Lord?

James, the half-brother of Jesus, was a kneeler. In fact, in addition to his nickname James the Just, given for his reputation for being a man of great justice and integrity, he also was known as "Old Camel Knees." In AD 325, Eusebius, a fourth-century historian, recorded several key events in the life of James, including an interesting tidbit about his knees:

> He alone was permitted to enter into the holy place; for he wore not woolen but linen garments. And he was in the habit of entering alone into the temple, and was frequently found upon his knees begging forgiveness for the people, so that his knees became hard like those of a camel, in consequence of his constantly bending them in his worship of God, and asking forgiveness for the people.[1]

Have you ever seen a camel's knees? Google them, and you'll see they're not that attractive! They are rough and calloused from bearing the weight of the camel when resting and getting up and down. No doubt James could relate. The vast amount of time he spent on his knees left a mark.

I hope the time you spend on your knees is leaving a mark too—not physically but in other ways. Prayer is one of the greatest gifts God has given us. It is a weapon to fight against evil. It is a bridge to connect to our heavenly Father and experience His love. It is a way to bring our requests before the God of the universe and to effect change.

Whatever is happening in your life, God is there, and through prayer He is ready to hear from you and speak to your heart. May your knees be "marked" from your time with the Lord this week!

Whatever is happening in your life, God is there, and through prayer He is ready to hear from you and speak to your heart.

PRAY

Find a posture of humility today (perhaps on your knees if you are physically able). Thank God for who He is and how He is continually ready to connect with you. (By the way, as I finish writing this, Sam is right here. Yet another reminder for me of how close God really is!)

DAY 4

SETTLE

Below you will find the Lord's Prayer from Matthew 6. Read through it multiple times, stopping to concentrate on each phrase as you ready your heart to focus on the Lord.

FOCUS

Are any of you suffering hardships? You should pray. Are any of you happy? You should sing praises. Are any of you sick? You should call for the elders of the church to come and pray over you, anointing you with oil in the name of the Lord. Such a prayer offered in faith will heal the sick, and the Lord will make you well. And if you have committed any sins, you will be forgiven.

Confess your sins to each other and pray for each other so that you may be healed. The earnest prayer of a righteous person has great power and produces wonderful results.

(James 5:13-16)

One day Jesus was praying in a certain place. When he finished, one of his disciples said to him, "Lord, teach us to pray."

(Luke 11:1 NIV)

"And when you pray, do not be like the hypocrites, for they love to pray standing in the synagogues and on the street corners to be seen by others. Truly I tell you, they have received their reward in full. But when you pray, go into your room, close the door and pray to your Father, who is unseen. Then your Father, who sees what is done in secret, will reward you. And when you pray, do not keep on babbling like pagans, for they think they will be heard because of their many words. Do not be like them, for your Father knows what you need before you ask him.

"This, then, is how you should pray:

"'Our Father in heaven,
hallowed be your name,
your kingdom come,
your will be done,
on earth as it is in heaven.
Give us today our daily bread.
And forgive us our debts,
as we also have forgiven our debtors.
And lead us not into temptation,
but deliver us from the evil one.'"

(Matthew 6:5-13 NIV)

REFLECT

Have you ever been intimidated to pray out loud? I have. At times, especially when around preachers and seminary professors, I have been nervous that I would be called on. In those moments you keep your head down, don't make eye contact, and maybe they will get the message. I begin to wonder, What if I stumble over my words or say something silly? Should I go King James style and throw in a *thee* and a *thou* for good measure? I don't want to mess it up. Or, if I'm honest, I don't want to be embarrassed.

But let me tell you, and remind myself, what a good prayer is. Prayer is simply an honest conversation between you and the one who loves you most. No fancy words required. In fact, sometimes the most honest prayer you can pray is very, very simple. Like, "Lord, help me," "Thank You, Jesus," "Please heal him, or "Show me Your will." These are simple prayers, but when prayed with a pure or sincere heart, they are powerful.

What is a powerful prayer? For me, it's one that gets results.

Reread James 5:16 (page 181). According to James, what brings powerful and wonderful results in prayer?

When have you cried out to God with an honest, earnest prayer? How did God respond?

Let's get practical today and address an important question: How do we pray effectively? If you're like me, sometimes your prayer life is active and vibrant. At other times, it feels ineffective and weak. How do we pray and develop a consistently powerful life of prayer?

Let's go to the expert, Jesus!

First, it's important to note that Jesus Himself spent a great deal of time in prayer. Repeatedly, we read how time spent communicating with God was a key component of Jesus's day-to-day life.

Consider these examples and note below each what you observe about Jesus's prayer life.

After he had dismissed the crowds, he went up on the mountain by himself to pray. When evening came, he was there alone.

(Matthew 14:23 ESV)

Early in the morning, while it was still dark, Jesus got up, left [the house], and went out to a secluded place, and was praying there.

(Mark 1:35 AMP)

Jesus Himself would often slip away to the wilderness to pray.

(Luke 5:16 NASB)

If the Son of God made prayer a priority, then how much more must we? Our first step in an effective and powerful life of prayer is to understand its necessity. Billy Graham once said, "Every man or woman whose life has counted for the church and the Kingdom of God has been a person of prayer. You cannot afford to be too busy to pray. A prayerless Christian is a powerless Christian."[2]

Prayer is a cornerstone of the Christian faith. It is an essential ingredient in the life of all believers who want to thrive. So, let's dig into how to pray in a way that pleases God and yields results!

In Luke 11:1, one of the disciples boldly asks Jesus how should we pray. In response, Jesus basically says, "This is how you should pray" and then shares what we have come to know as the Lord's Prayer. We see this exchange recorded in both Luke 11 and Matthew 6.

Let's take a closer look at this famous prayer and dissect it to establish the key elements laid out by Jesus.

Our Father, which art in heaven, Hallowed be thy name.
(Matthew 6:9b KJV)

Hallowed is not a term often used in modern society, but it is a term of consecration, meaning the One who is set apart and holy above all. This opening phrase is an acknowledgment of God's holiness.

Thy kingdom come, Thy will be done in earth, as it is in heaven.
(Matthew 6:10 KJV)

This portion of the prayer is also a statement of faith. It acknowledges first that God will return and that one day all will be set right in this world.

> **Prayer is a cornerstone of the Christian faith. It is an essential ingredient in the life of all believers who want to thrive.**

That is not the case currently, as we all can attest. We live in a fallen world. Sin is rampant. Does God's will always prevail? No! But one day it will. When God's kingdom comes, His will will be done perfectly here, just as it is now in heaven. This phrase of the prayer is a yearning for that day. In addition to the coming kingdom, this part of the prayer can be a petition for God's kingdom to reign within us and our lives.

> *Give us this day our daily bread.*
> *(Matthew 6:11 KJV)*

Notice the word *us* here. I love that as Jesus teaches His disciples to pray, the emphasis is not just on ourselves but on the body of believers. Give us, the community of faith, what we need on a daily basis. It is a corporate request to God on behalf of all believers.

> *And forgive us our debts, as we forgive our debtors.*
> *(Matthew 6:12 KJV)*

This sentence is power-packed. First, we are to confess our sins. Again, the word *us* is used. There is a sense that as the people of God, we have an obligation to corporately repent. Yet there also is an intimacy in this phrase. It is personal. It's not only for the body but also for the individual to confess their sins and lay them before God in repentance.

Then the second phrase takes it a step further. In the same way we want to be forgiven, we are to forgive others. Both confessing our sins and forgiving those who hurt us are required for the effective prayer life.

> *And lead us not into temptation, but deliver us from evil: For thine is the kingdom, and the power, and the glory, for ever. Amen.*
> *(Matthew 6:13 KJV)*

Jesus ends with a prayer for protection. Again, notice the word *us*. There is a sense that as the family of God we are in this together. His example teaches that we are a body working as one, and therefore we should pray not only for our own protection from the schemes of Satan but also for all who follow Christ everywhere.

Take the time to write the Lord's Prayer, phrase by phrase, in your own words here:

As we read through this portion of James, it is important to be reminded once again of the context. For believers in the first-century church, it was a tough environment in which to live. They faced many hardships and challenges. I imagine they clung to this model of prayer. Communicating with God, pouring their hearts out and then listening for His response, must have been a daily way of sustaining themselves through their trials.

It can be the same for us. Life can be challenging. If we want to truly thrive in our faith, an active prayer life is foundational.

PRAY

As you go through the day, repeat the Lord's Prayer multiple times—silently or aloud. Ask God to reveal ways in which you can strengthen your connection to Him through prayer.

DAY 5

SETTLE

Reflect on how God has been with you during difficult seasons of your life and spend time thanking Him. You may want to sing a song of praise or simply pray "Thank you, Jesus" for all the ways He has been with you throughout your life, especially in the struggles.

FOCUS

Therefore confess your sins to each other and pray for each other so that you may be healed. The prayer of a righteous person is powerful and effective.

Elijah was a human being, even as we are. He prayed earnestly that it would not rain, and it did not rain on the land for three and a half years. Again he prayed, and the heavens gave rain, and the earth produced its crops.

My brothers and sisters, if one of you should wander from the truth and someone should bring that person back, remember this: Whoever turns a sinner from the error of their way will save them from death and cover over a multitude of sins.

(James 5:16-20 NIV)

REFLECT

For six weeks we have traveled through a power-packed letter written by the half-brother of Jesus. James, as the leader of the first-century church, wanted to give his fellow disciples sound teaching and encouragement to face life with wisdom and peace despite the difficult circumstances in which they lived. This short book reads like the Proverbs of the New Testament, offering practical teaching and tools to help the reader succeed in everyday life. These instructions can help us learn to thrive as followers of Christ today!

Through this study we have spent time focusing on six major themes from James's writing: Endurance, Wisdom, Action, Control, Humility, and Prayer. Each of these is integral in developing a mature and Christlike character.

How did you do with the weekly memory verses? Just for fun, try to complete these passages.

Week 1: James 1:2-3—When troubles of any...

Week 2: James 1:5—If you need wisdom...

Week 3: James 1:22—But don't just listen...

Week 4: James 1:26—If you claim to be...

Week 5: James 4:7—So humble yourselves before...

Week 6: James 5:16—The earnest prayer...

How'd you do with completing the Scriptures? I hope you aced it, but if not, no problem! Make yourself some note cards and put them in prominent places where you will see them often. It may be easier to learn them that way. These are definitely words to live by!

As James draws his letter to a close, his focus moves to two very heavy topics: confession and restoration:

Confess your sins to each other…

you can be sure that whoever brings the sinner back from wandering will save that person from death and bring about the forgiveness of many sins.

(James 5:16, 20)

James, in his usual fashion, has a no-nonsense way of writing. So, ending his letter with a command to do the hard work of the faith is on brand. After all, what is harder than dealing with our own sins and then restoring others caught in the same?

Let's take these one at a time. First, there is the practice of admitting our sins to other trusted believers.

Confess your sins to each other.
(James 5:16)

What thoughts and emotions do you have when you read this statement?

Let me be honest here—this makes me uncomfortable. I don't really want to confess my sins, my inadequacies, my failures to anyone but God. And even with Him, it's sometimes uncomfortable. But telling someone else? That's scary. What will people think? Will they gossip about me? Can they be trusted? These are questions that run through my mind.

And since we are being honest, we may also think, How bad are my sins anyway? It's just not that a big of a deal. I can handle this between me and God.

What are your primary hesitations when it comes to confessing your sins to another person?

Though we might want to keep our sins just between us and God, James tells us we have to go a step further by confessing our sins to another trusted believer.

Confession of sins is a toughie! Our society teaches us to be strong. Admitting our faults, on the other hand, is seen to show failure and weakness. These are not highly sought out qualities. Plus, life teaches us that we had better be careful who we trust. You have probably had the experience of sharing something you thought was held in confidence only to find out that your confidant was a blabbermouth. That hurts. In fact, it can be devastating—so much so that you may decide trusting is something you will never do again. I've been there—I get it!

But (you knew there was a but coming, didn't you?) God's word tells us that in the confession of sins there is growth. In fact, James says that through confession there is healing! That's a great promise. Developing a few close friends who can serve as your confidants and encouragers will help you become the best version of who God created you to be. Without those people it is like you are flying on a trapeze without a net. You need someone there to catch you when you fall, and you will fall, friend. Developing a small network of people who will hold you accountable can give you a net for a soft landing. Then, after the fall, if those people are good friends, they will help you get back on solid ground.

Who are the mature believers in whom you can confide?

> **God's word tells us that in the confession of sins there is growth.**

How can you intentionally develop these relationships?

What sins do you need to confess today?

Now, let's look at the last sentence of James's letter—a call to help restore those who fall away in their faith.

If someone among you wanders away from the truth and is brought back, you can be sure that whoever brings the sinner back from wandering will save that person.

(James 5:19-20)

What thoughts and emotions do you have when you read this statement?

In theory, that sounds great, right? You love God. You love other people. When other people get it wrong, you can help them out by gently pointing it out so they can get back on track. What could possibly go wrong? Ha! This is good in theory, but it's tough in execution. In general, people don't like it when others point out their sins. But if we want to bring about restoration, we have to find a way to do it anyway with love, gentleness, and grace.

Restoring others in faith requires wisdom, patience, a tender heart, tough skin, and lots of prayer. Knowing what to say and where to say it is crucial. Tone and timing also count. As you take on this role as a person of faith, do it with God's leading and filled with love.

And remember this: Real love is willing to go on the rescue mission. Shallow love watches from the shore as others drown. Shallow love takes no risk. It observes from a safe distance and watches as others go under. But real love does the hard thing!

Who in your life has demonstrated real love by doing the hard thing on your behalf?

Rescue missions are a noble task. When someone in your life wanders away from God, don't let it happen easily. As believers, we are family. And healthy families show up for one another. It's what we do. So, pray and ask God what you can do.

This brings us back to our theme of the week, prayer. If you have people in your life who have wandered away from God, or from God's standards, your first step is prayer. Don't make them your spiritual project. Instead, make them the focus of prayer. Ask God to guide you in how and when to approach them in a winsome and loving way so that your words will be God's words and your attitude that of Christ. And then hope and pray that their response will be one that pleases the Holy Spirit.

Whom do you know needs rescuing from sin?

Are you willing to be used by God to help restore them? If not, what is holding you back?

Talk with God about any hesitancies or concerns you have and listen for what God has to say. What is God's invitation?

James leaves us with a call to prayer that ends with a call to the actions of confession and restoration. When we think about it, this is also the message of Christ. Through the confession of our sins and belief in Jesus, we receive what was done for us through the cross. And that restores us into a right relationship with God. This is the story of Jesus.

Church history tells us that James eventually gave his life for the cause of Christ. The half-brother who once mocked Jesus became the leader of the first-century church and ultimately gave his life in its service. His letter was written to help believers then and now to thrive. And this is my hope for you as well. Friends, I pray that you would *thrive*!

PRAY

As we close out our study, may I pray for you?

Lord, may the woman reading these words become strong and brave and true in Christ. Give her a life that is filled with wisdom, truth, and joy. May she have a boldness to live in ways that bring a smile to Your face and that make a difference in this world. We love You, Jesus. Help us become more and more like You. Amen.

Through the confession of our sins and belief in Jesus, we receive what was done for us through the cross.

Prayer

Exercising the Power Tool of the Faith

The earnest prayer of a righteous person has great power and produces wonderful results.

(James 5:16b)

Prayers offered in faith and in line with God's will can do amazing things. Here are three steps:

1. Be _____.

2. Be _____.

3. Be _____.

The _____, _____, and _____ prayers of righteous people can _____ the _____!

Chapter
Summaries

THE
BOOK
OF
JAMES

AUTHOR AND BACKGROUND

Who better to write to early believers than the guy who grew up with Jesus and then found himself a key leader of the early church? As the half-brother of Jesus, James was uniquely qualified to share his insights and practical wisdom with the first-century Christians. Written between AD 45–49, this short five-chapter letter reads like the Proverbs of the New Testament. His crisp and concise writing gives the reader clear direction about living in ways that please God. In these 108 verses James tackles tough topics such as faith, good works, controlling our words, and prayer.

CHAPTER SUMMARIES AND KEY VERSES

Week 1

The church, which originally had been concentrated in Jerusalem, began to scatter abroad as persecution began. James emerged as the primary leader. He begins his letter by encouraging believers to endure their hardships as an opportunity to grow in their faith. His instructions include praying for wisdom, enduring hardships patiently, and being very careful not to give into temptations when times are difficult. This first chapter gives the practical instruction to be sure that actions and beliefs line up and that all believers are careful with their words.

KEY VERSES (NIV)

James 1:2-3—*Consider it pure joy, my brothers and sisters, whenever you face trials of many kinds, because you know that the testing of your faith produces perseverance.*

James 1:5—*If any of you lacks wisdom, you should ask God, who gives generously to all without finding fault, and it will be given to you.*

James 1:19b—*Everyone should be quick to listen, slow to speak and slow to become angry.*

James 1:22—*Do not merely listen to the word, and so deceive yourselves. Do what it says.*

James 1:26—Those who consider themselves religious and yet do not keep a tight rein on their tongues deceive themselves, and their religion is worthless.

James 1:27a—Religion that God our Father accepts as pure and faultless is this: to look after orphans and widows in their distress.

Week 2

The second chapter of James focuses on the theme of putting our faith into action and argues against showing favoritism and prejudice in any forms. The bulk of this section of the letter helps the reader understand that faith without works, to use James's words, is useless. Believing and being about God's work go hand in hand. Christianity is not a theory to be embraced but a relationship to be lived out in devotion to God as expressed in love toward Him and others.

KEY VERSES (NIV)

James 2:1—My brothers and sisters, believers in our glorious Lord Jesus Christ must not show favoritism.

James 2:14—What good is it, my brothers and sisters, if someone claims to have faith but has no deeds? Can such faith save them?

James 2:17b—Faith by itself, if it is not accompanied by action, is dead.

Week 3

As James continues, he focuses on the power of words. By comparing our tongue to a bit in a horse's mouth, a rudder on a ship, and a spark that causes a forest fire, he vividly illustrates how dangerous words can be when used carelessly. What we do and what we say have consequences and are a representation of who we are in Christ. James continues in verses 13-28 by describing the character traits of those who are wise by God's standards: pure, peace loving, gentle, impartial, sincere, and full of mercy and good deeds.

Key Verses (NIV)

James 3:2—We all stumble in many ways. Anyone who is never at fault in what they say is perfect, able to keep their whole body in check.

James 3:5—The tongue is a small part of the body, but it makes great boasts. Consider what a great forest is set on fire by a small spark.

James 3:13—Who is wise and understanding among you? Let them show it by their good life, by deeds done in the humility that comes from wisdom.

James 3:17—But the wisdom that comes from heaven is first of all pure; then peace-loving, considerate, submissive, full of mercy and good fruit, impartial and sincere.

Week 4

This chapter continues the theme of chapter 3 of seeking God's standards and not our own. James identifies worldliness and selfishness as primary causes of problems within the church. He instructs us to humble ourselves before God in order to receive honor. The chapter ends with a warning against self-righteous attitudes and critical spirits.

Key Verses (NIV)

James 4:1-2—What causes fights and quarrels among you? Don't they come from your desires that battle within you? You desire but do not have, so you kill. You covet but you cannot get what you want, so you quarrel and fight. You do not have because you do not ask God.

James 4:3-4—When you ask, you do not receive, because you ask with wrong motives, that you may spend what you get on your pleasures.

James 4:7—Submit yourselves, then, to God. Resist the devil, and he will flee from you. Come near to God and he will come near to you.

James 4:10—Humble yourselves before the Lord, and he will lift you up.

James 4:17—If anyone, then, knows the good they ought to do and doesn't do it, it is sin for them.

Week 5

James ends this practical letter with three distinct themes: (1) a warning to the rich of this world not to trust in possessions or abuse those under your direction; (2) encouragement to be patient in sufferings and struggles, trusting that God is in control and will reward those who trust in Him; and (3) an exhortation to pray in all things, whether they be struggles, celebrations, sickness, or confession. The appropriate response is always prayer.

KEY VERSES (NIV)

James 5:9—Don't grumble against one another, brothers and sisters, or you will be judged. The Judge is standing at the door!

James 5:13-15a—Is anyone among you in trouble? Let them pray. Is anyone happy? Let them sing songs of praise. Is anyone among you sick? Let them call the elders of the church to pray over them and anoint them with oil in the name of the Lord. And the prayer offered in faith will make the sick person well.

James 5:16—Therefore confess your sins to each other and pray for each other so that you may be healed. The prayer of a righteous person is powerful and effective.

James 5:20—Remember this: Whoever turns a sinner from the error of their way will save them from death and cover over a multitude of sins.

Video Viewer Guide: ANSWERS

Week 1

thrive / prospering/ flourishing

prepare

if / when

Week 2

grow older/ growing up

separates

Wisdom

draw close

do

Week 3

Possible answers for blanks 1–3:
Each created for a unique purpose /
work together / productive / help the
world around them thrive / produce
something wonderful.

action

faithful/ good deeds

Week 4

Decide

Immerse

Ask

Week 5

less/ but/ less

examine

Humble

Resist

Week 6

sincere

faithful

relentless

sincere / faithful/ relentless /
change / world

Notes

Week 1: Endurance

1. The fact that James's name always appears first in lists in Scripture suggests that he was the eldest of Jesus's siblings.
2. C. S. Lewis, *Mere Christianity* (Nashville, TN: Broadman and Holman Publishers, 1980), 56.
3. Bill Potter, "Nero's Persecutions Begin, July 24, A.D. 64 (or 67)," Landmark Events, July 22, 2019, https://landmarkevents.org/neros-persecutions-begin-a-d-64/.

Week 2: Wisdom

1. Proverbs is a collection of wisdom coming from a variety of sources, though traditionally it is believed that Solomon wrote a major portion of the wise sayings. The author of Ecclesiastes identifies himself in Ecclesiastes 1:1 as Qoheleth, meaning "Preacher." Traditionally Qoheleth has been identified as Solomon, though there is debate among scholars. Similarly, traditionally Song of Solomon has been attributed to Solomon, though there is some debate among scholars today.

Week 3: Action

1. George Whitefield, *Eighteen sermons preached by the late Rev. George Whitefield, A.M. on the following subjects ... Taken verbatim in short-hand, and faithfully transcribed by Joseph Gurney; revised by Andrew Gifford, D.D.* (Newburyport, MA: Edmund M. Blunt., 1797; Ann Arbor: Text Creation Partnership, 2011), "Sermon XVII: Jacob's Ladder," p. 333. https://quod.lib.umich.edu/cgi/t/text/pageviewer-idx?cc=evans;c=evans;idno=n25065.0001.001;node=N25065.0001.001:19;seq=341;page=root;view=text.
2. Billy Graham, *Hope for Each Day: Words of Wisdom and Faith* (Nashville: Thomas Nelson, 2017), 12.

Week 4: Control

1. Brandon Showater, "Was Jesus a Carpenter or Stone Mason?" Metro Voice, October 11, 2018, https://metrovoicenews.com/was-jesus-a-carpenter-or-stone-mason/.

Week 5: Humility

1. "Humility," Augnet, Augnet.org/en/works-of-augustine/his-ideas/2313-humility/, accessed December 12, 2022.

Week 6: Prayer

1. Matt Erickson, "Old Camel Knees: A Brief Reflection on the Remarkable Prayer Life of James the Just," Renovate, August 29, 2019, https://mwerickson.com/2019/08/29/old-camel-knees-a-brief-reflection-on-the-remarkable-prayer-life-of-james-the-just/.
2. "Day by Day with Billy Graham: Prayer Is a Conversation," YouVersion, https://www.bible.com/reading-plans/601-the-billy-graham-devo/day/182, accessed December 19, 2022.

(Copyright page continued from page 4.)

More Bible Studies from Jennifer Cowart

Learn from the fierce women of God who changed the world.
Fierce: Women of the Bible Who Changed the World

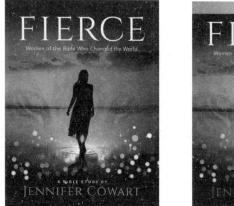

Participant Workbook | 9781501882906

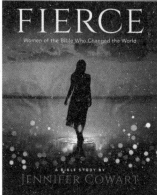

Leader Guide | 9781501882920

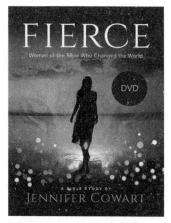

Video-DVD | 9781501882944

The word *fierce* is trendy. It is used to describe women who are extreme athletes, high-level executives, or supermodels. Women at the top of their game. But what about the rest of us? Can we be fierce? Absolutely! In fact, women like us have been changing the world for thousands of years—many who received little fanfare yet lived fiercely anyway. In this six-week study we will look at lesser-known female characters in the Bible and the ways they changed the world by living into God's calling, including:

- The midwives of Egypt (Shiphrah and Puah), who made hard decisions in the face of evil
- Deborah, who was an unlikely and powerful leader
- Naaman's slave girl, who bravely points others to God's healing power
- The Woman at the Well, who boldly repented and shared her faith
- Lois and Eunice, who parented with intentionality and effectiveness
- Dorcas, who showed kindness to those in need.

As we explore their lives, we will discover how we too can live into our callings, honor the Lord, and even change the world through our courage, faithfulness, and obedience.

Explore excerpts and video teaching samples at AbingdonWomen.com.

Abingdon *Women*

More Bible Studies from Jennifer Cowart

God can turn your messy life into a masterpiece.
Messy People: Life Lessons from Imperfect Biblical Heroes

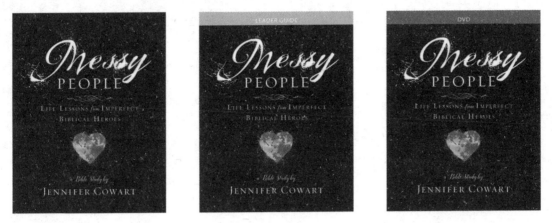

Participant Workbook | 9781501863127   Leader Guide | 9781501863141   Video-DVD | 9781501863165

Every life gets messy at times. Sometimes these messes are literal, like a house that would be easier to condemn than to clean. But sometimes they are intangible messes such as illness, conflict, depression, abuse, bankruptcy, divorce, and job loss. And these messes can be painful, hurting our hearts and our homes. But as we see in the Bible, God loves to use messy people!

In this six-week study, we will dig into the lives of biblical heroes who were messy people just like us but who were used by God in powerful ways.

Together we will examine the stories of five wonderful but messy people and one messy parable character:

- Rahab
- The Prodigal Son
- Josiah
- Mary
- David
- Daniel

From their stories, we will learn how God can use broken people, restore damaged hearts and relationships, give us power to handle our critics, and help us deal with the hard moments of life. Along the way we'll discover that we don't have to just endure messy lives but can actually learn to thrive with God's guidance and help. In the hands of God, our messes can become His masterpieces!

Explore excerpts and video teaching samples at AbingdonWomen.com.

WATCH VIDEOS BASED ON
THRIVE:
LIVING FAITHFULLY IN DIFFICULT TIMES
WITH JENNIFER COWART THROUGH AMPLIFY MEDIA.

Amplify Media is a multimedia platform that delivers high-quality, searchable content with an emphasis on Wesleyan perspectives for churchwide, group, or individual use on any device at any time. In a world of sometimes overwhelming choices, Amplify gives church leaders and congregants media capabilities that are contemporary, relevant, effective, and, most important, affordable and sustainable.

With *Amplify Media* church leaders can:

- Provide a reliable source of Christian content through a Wesleyan lens for teaching, training, and inspiration in a customizable library
- Deliver their own preaching and worship content in a way the congregation knows and appreciates
- Build the church's capacity to innovate with engaging content and accessible technology
- Equip the congregation to better understand the Bible and its application
- Deepen discipleship beyond the church walls

Ask your group leader or pastor about Amplify Media
and sign up today at www.AmplifyMedia.com.